James Richmond Sheen

**Wines and Other Fermented Liquors**

From the Earliest Ages to the Present Time

James Richmond Sheen

**Wines and Other Fermented Liquors**
*From the Earliest Ages to the Present Time*

ISBN/EAN: 9783337184254

Printed in Europe, USA, Canada, Australia, Japan

Cover: Foto ©Andreas Hilbeck / pixelio.de

More available books at **www.hansebooks.com**

# WINES

AND

## OTHER FERMENTED LIQUORS;

FROM THE

### 𝕰arliest 𝕬ges to the present 𝕿ime.

DEDICATED TO

## ALL CONSUMERS IN THE UNITED KINGDOM.

BY

# JAMES RICHMOND SHEEN.

" If it be true that a wise man, like a good refiner, can gather gold out of the drossiest volume, and that a fool will be a fool with the best book,—yea, or without a book ; there is no reason that we should deprive a wise man of any advantage to his wisdom, while we seek to restrain from a fool that which, being restrained, will be no hindrance to his folly."—MILTON'S 'AREOPAGITICA,' sec. 28. (1644.)

LONDON:

ROBERT HARDWICKE, 192, PICCADILLY. W.

AND ALL BOOKSELLERS.

" But ' why then publish ? ' There are no rewards
  Of fame or profit when the world grows weary.
I ask in turn,—Why do you play at cards ?
  Why drink? why read?—To make some hour less dreary.
It occupies me to turn back regards
  On what I've seen or pondered, sad or cheery ;
And what I write I cast upon the stream
To swim or sink."

BYRON.    ' Don Juan,' canto xiv, st. 11.

# PREFACE.

N inscribing this volume to "All Consumers in the United Kingdom," the Author can scarcely be accused of offering the incense of adulation at any particular shrine; at the same time he trusts he may stand acquitted of presumption in thus casting his little bark upon the waters without invoking the prestige of some known authority, under the shadow of whose mantle its defects might possibly pass unheeded, and whose sanction might probably prove a passport to obtain for it a more favourable notice.

Several works have, at different times, been written on the article of Wine; those of ancient date are almost obsolete and ill-adapted for the requirements of the present day; whilst those of modern issue are published at a high price, and, although sufficiently voluminous on the subject of wines, do not treat of other fermented drinks. Although these latter may not date their origin from a period equally as remote, their history may, nevertheless, not be altogether uninteresting to the general reader.

To supply this requisite, and in as small compass as possible, the Author respectfully presumes to invite attention to his brief treatise on 'Wines, and other Fermented Liquors;' trusting it will be found to possess sufficient interest to render it worthy of an attentive and candid perusal.

*Upper St. Martin's Lane, London.*
*December,* 1864.

# CONTENTS.

## CHAPTER I.     PAGE

*Historical Account of the Wines of the Ancients.*

Antiquity of wine. Wines of the ancients. Time for
keeping. The *fumarium.* Wine vessels found at
Herculaneum and Pompeii. The *rhyton.* The
*amphora.* The *patera.* Roman cellars in upper
rooms. Wine cart    .    .    .    .    I

## CHAPTER II.

*Early History of the Vine.*

Earliest account of the vine. Its native countries.
Size of the Syrian grapes. The vine brought to
Italy, France, and Spain. Its further progress   .   8

## CHAPTER III.

*Vineyards in this Country.*

The vine introduced into England by the Romans.
Vineyards in the vale of Gloucester. Religious
houses in southern and western counties had their
vineyards. Produce of a vineyard at Arundel
Castle. Vineyard at Kensington. Champagne
the growth of a vineyard at Cobham    .    .   12

## CHAPTER IV.

*Climates suitable to the Vine.*

Importance of solar heat. Variation of temperature.
Area of wine culture. Different species of the
grape, and innumerable varieties    .    .   15

*b*

## CHAPTER V.

### *Culture of the Vine.*

Soil best adapted to the vine. Importance of favourable aspect. Vegetable manures. Forcing a recent introduction. Vineries. Productiveness of the vine. Age it attains . . . . 18

## CHAPTER VI.

### *Vineyards of France and Italy.*

Mode of planting in France. Manner of staking down the vine. Its stunted appearance. The vineyards of Italy. Mode of training the vines. Their picturesque appearance. Description of gathering the fruit. Profusion of grapes. Left unpicked on the vines. Indolence of the natives . 23

## CHAPTER VII.

### *Wine chemically considered.*

Vinous fermentation. Presence of tartar. Juice of the grape and other wines. Adulteration of wines. To give them strength. To change or perfect their colour. To remove their acidity. Employment of lead. Tests to denote its presence. Brande's table. Fortifying wines. Fretting in. Constituents of wine . . . . 31

## CHAPTER VIII.

### *Wine considered in relation to health and disease.*

Wine useful or prejudicial greatly dependent on its perfect fermentation. The temperate use of good wine recommended. Plato. Anatomy of Melancholy. Dr. Sandford. Dr. Holdsworth. Dr. McCulloch. Dr. Brinton. Dr. Pereira. Dr. Paris. Effervescent wines recommended in great prostration of strength. Van Swieten. Invalids should avoid mixing wines. The generous use of wine . 38

## CHAPTER IX.

PAGE

*Authors who have written on the subject of Wine.*

Wine a popular theme with writers. Homer. Anacreon. Phocylides. Mago. Columella. Democritus. Plato. Aristotle. Hippocrates. Galen. Cato. Sea-water used in wine making. Varro. Cicero. Virgil. Tibullus. Horace. Martial. Juvenal. Ovid. Zeno. Pliny. Erasmus. Patin. Paumier. Lord Bacon. Andrea Baccius. Sir Edward Barry. Dr. Henderson. Cyrus Redding. Dr. Mc Culloch. Busby. Chaptal. Jullien. Paguierre. Forrester. Tovey. Shaw. Denman. Bronner. Scham. Graff . . . 44

## CHAPTER X.

*General arrangement and classification of Wines.*

Sweet wines. Sparkling wines. Dry and light wines. Dry and strong wines. Classification . . 52

## CHAPTER XI.

*On the Wines of France.*

Division of France for fiscal purposes. Extent of vineyard ground. Value and quantity of wine produced. Wine growers. The Gironde. Value of wine estates. Médoc wines. The Côtes wines. Origin of the vineyards of Hermitage. Burgundy district. A French luncheon. Produce of the vineyards of Burgundy. Present of wine to Charles II. Duties formerly charged. The Methuen treaty. Introduction of the red wine of Portugal. Equalization of duty in 1831. Present scale of duties. Objections, and why. Arguments to the same effect. Testimony of dealers. Dispute respecting Burgundy and Champagne. Champagne. Pressings. The *bouquet*. Bottling.

PAGE

Bursting of bottles. *Dégorgement.* The crémant
wines. *Cuvées* at Rheims. Champagne in cases
of great prostration. Injured by icing. Should
be placed side downwards. The muscadine wines.
The *oidium. Halle aux Vins.* Good wine needs
no bush . . . . . 56

## CHAPTER XII.

### *On the Wines of Spain.*

Geographical position. Climate. Wines of Xeres.
Large stocks. Wines of Montilla. Uncertainty
as to Sack. Opinions thereon. Ballads in praise
of. Scarcity of rain. Wine cheaper than water.
Innkeeper at Ravenna. The *oidium.* Increased
consumption of Sherry . . . . 91

## CHAPTER XIII.

### *On the Wines of Portugal.*

Geographical position. Natural advantages. The
Methuen treaty. Verses in derision of Port. Deep
potations. Curious will. Adulteration of Port.
A word in its defence. Port made to order.
Genuine wine unsaleable. Scenery of the Douro.
Lodges at Villa Nova. The *oidium.* Description
of Lisbon. Its *quintas.* Increased consumption
of Port . . . . . 107

## CHAPTER XIV.

### *On the Wines of Madeira, the Canaries, &c.*

Climate of Madeira. Vineyards first planted. Over
shipment. The *oidium.* Introduction of vines
from America. The Canaries. Peak of Teneriffe.
Abundant vegetation. Howell's eulogium on
Canary wine. Peruvian Madeira. Jurors' Report. 128

## CHAPTER XV.

*On the Wines of Germany, Hungary, Austria, and Switzerland.* PAGE

Vineyards of Germany. Their antiquity questioned. The Rheingau. Scenery of the Rhine. Soil and climate. Rhine wines. Wine sale in 1836. High price. Wines of the Palatinate. Bavarian Stein wines. Wine auction at Wurzburg. The Nahe. Wines of the Moselle. The Saar. Sparkling wines. Wines of the Tyrol. Curative properties of German wines. Jurors' Report. Wines of Hungary. Supply much in excess of demand. Fancy price of Tokay. Defective manipulation. Jurors' Report. Wines of Austria. Their excellent quality. Perfectness and great freedom from spirit. Their keeping properties. The vineyards. Favourable opinions respecting these wines. Jurors' Report. Wines of Switzerland. Jurors' Report. 140

## CHAPTER XVI.

*On the Wines of Italy, Sicily, and Sardinia.*

Wines of Italy. Their decadence. Capabilities of production. Careless manipulation. The *oidium.* Wines of Sicily. Decreased consumption. Wines of Sardinia. Jurors' Report . . . 164

## CHAPTER XVII.

*On the Wines of Greece, Ionian Islands, Persia, Turkish Provinces, and the Crimea.*

Wines of Greece. Homer's Nectar. Wines of Candia and Cyprus. Islands of the Archipelago. Cos. Isle of Rhodes. Ionian Islands. Wines of Ithaca. The Greeks deep drinkers. The Morea.

PAGE

Greek modern wines inferior to those of old. Degeneracy, and how accounted for. Wines of Persia. Smyrna. Island of Tenedos. Plains of Troy. Syria. Its wines. The Crimea. The vine introduced. Excellence of the wines. Jurors' Report . . . . . 173

## CHAPTER XVIII.

### *On the Wines of America and California.*

Wines of America. The vines indigenous. Increase of the vineyards. Wine more extensively made. Great freedom from alcohol. Lines in praise of Catawba. California. Its wines. Wine growing on the increase . . . . 188

## CHAPTER XIX.

### *On the Wines of the British Colonies and Settlements.*

Cape of Good Hope. Vines first planted. Cape wines. Used for mixing with better wines. Statistics. Australia. Geographical position. Vine planting. Expectations scarcely realized. Jurors' Report . . . . . 195

## CHAPTER XX.

### *A few passing remarks on Wines.*

Bad wines. Treaty of 1862. French and Spanish Reds. Hamburg Sherry. Extract from ' Medical Times and Gazette.' Extract from ' Ridley's Circular.' Report of Commissioners of Customs. Other opinions in confirmation. The " Family Grocer." Amusing quotation. Qualifications of a wine merchant. Advice to buyers. Statistical returns . . . . . 203

## CHAPTER XXI.

*On the Cellar and General Management of Wines.*

Importance of the cellar. Its situation. Arrangement of. Iron bins. Their superiority. Wine
keeps better in large casks than small. Great tun
of Heidelberg. Size of casks. Racking. Fining.
Bottling. Small bottles. Packing cases serving as
cellarets. Wine cooling an ancient practice.
Icing wines. Decanting . . . 218

## CHAPTER XXII.

*History and Antiquity of Malt Liquors.*

Antiquity of brewing. Beer of the Egyptians. Of
the Gauls. Of the ancient Germans. German
beer largely imported. Prohibitory duty laid on.
Saxon dialogues. Brewhouses attached to the
monasteries. Old ballad. Price and quality of
beer regulated by Parliament. Ale conners . 237

## CHAPTER XXIII.

*On the Art of Brewing.*

Process of brewing. Improvements in. The various
stages of. The fermentation the most important
operation. Origin of porter . . . 245

## CHAPTER XXIV.

*Some Account of Barley and Malt.*

Malting. Quantity made. Barley. Its different
varieties. Two crops in the same year. Barley
restricted to the purpose of food in times of
scarcity . . . . . 250

### CHAPTER XXV.

*Some Account of Hops.* PAGE

The hop. Indigenous to this country. Hops imported from Flanders. The hop first cultivated in England. Its management. Repeal of the duty. 254

### CHAPTER XXVI.

*Opinions on Malt Liquors, medical and otherwise.*

Beer and ale. Proportion of alcohol in. Medical opinions. Beer a national beverage. The questions of prohibition and permissive use considered. Export beers . . . . . 260

### CHAPTER XXVII.

*On Distillation and Rectification.*

Distillation not known to the ancients. First mentioned. Rectification . . . . 268

### CHAPTER XXVIII.

*On British and Foreign Spirits.*

Spirits. Description and statistics of. Compounds. Liqueurs. Ancient mode of testing the strength of spirits . . . . . 275

### CHAPTER XXIX.

*Conclusion.*

Concluding address. Valedictory . . 283

# CHAPTER I.

---

An Historical Account of the Wines
of the Ancients.

" Not a tree,
A plant, a leaf, a blossom, but contains
A folio volume."—Hurdis. ' *Evening Walk*.'

---

INES and other fermented liquors
were known in the most remote
ages of antiquity. The Sacred Historian
tells us, that, after the flood (which is supposed to have occurred 2348 years before
Christ), " Noah planted a vineyard ; and
he drank of the wine, and was drunken."
(*Genesis* ix, 20, 21.) Homer, the most ancient of all the profane writers whose works
have reached us, and who lived more than
900 years before the Christian era, frequently

B

mentions wine, bestowing on it the epithet
"divine;" and notices its effects on the
mind and body. (*Odyssey, Books* ix.-xxi.)
"The wines of the ancients," Chaptal observes, "were so concentrated by means of
heat, that they rather deserve the name of
extracts or syrups than of wines; they must
have been very sweet, and but little fermented; apparently, to remedy this, they
were kept for a great length of time."
According to Aristotle and Galen, seven
years was the shortest period necessary for
keeping wine before it was fit to drink, but
wines of a century old were not uncommon
at the tables of the luxurious citizens of
ancient Rome; and Horace boasts of his
drinking *Falernian,* born as it were with
him, or which reckoned its age from the
same consuls.

"O nata mecum consule Manlio."—*Ode* xxi, *book* 3.

Indeed the odes of Horace abound with
manifestations of the same taste, thus,—

"I pete——
Et Cadum Marsi memoram duelli."
*Ode* xxiv, *book* 3.

Here Horace sends his slave for a vessel of the wine on which the Marian war was recorded, and which must therefore have been sixty-eight years old. We may here remark that it was the practice in those days not only to inscribe on the vessel the age of the wine, but likewise to chronicle thereon the date of any remarkable event of subsequent occurrence. Again, in *Ode* xxviii. *book* 3, we find Horace calling for

" Bibuli Consulis amphoram."

Now as the poet was born in the Consulate of Manlius, as above stated, which happened in the year B.C. 65, and Bibullus was Consul in 59 B.C., the wine must have been hoarded from the time Horace was six years of age. Pliny is very precise as to the time which wine may be kept advantageously :—

" Non alia res majus incrementum sentit ad vigesimum annum, majusve ab eo dispendium."—*Book* xiv, *c.* 4.

Cicero, in his ' Brutus,' disapproves of very old wine :—

"Nimia vetustas nec habet eam quam quærimus suavitatem, nec est jam sane tolerabilis."—*c.* 83.

Plautus compares old wine which has lost its relish and strength, to a man who has lost his teeth by age :—

" Vinum vetustate edentulum."
'*Pœnulus,*' *Act* iii, *Sc.* iii, *v.* 37.

The wines of the ancients have been described as " thick and fat," owing to their having been evaporated in the *fumarium* to a consolidated state, so that they could not be poured out of the vessel until dissolved by hot water. The proof is recorded in Horace :—

" Amphoræ fumum bibere institutæ."
*Ode* iii, *book* 8.

Tibullus also alludes to it :—

" Nunc mihi fumosos veteris proferte Falernos."
*Ode* ii, *book* 1, *v.* 27.

Andrea Baccius, in his work " De Naturali Vinorum Historia" (A.D. 1596), speaking of the wines in Alsace, says that they were exposed to the smoke in hot chambers, where they became so thick that they were no longer drinkable, unless they were beaten with twigs, or diluted with hot water.

During the excavations at Herculaneum and Pompeii, there were found among the ruins vases which had been used for the inspissation of the fluid, and in which traces of the wine were deposited in a crystallized state. The earthen vessel used by the Greeks and Romans to contain their wines was called the *amphora*. It received its name from its two ears or handles. It is generally from two to three feet in height; and the body ending upwards with a short neck, tapers towards the lower part almost to a point. Earthern amphoræ of the Roman time have been occasionally found in England, and various specimens are to be met with in the Elgin and Townley Galleries of the British Museum.

RHYTON,
or Drinking Horn.

AMPHORA,
or Earthen Wine Holder.

PATERA,
or Drinking Cup.

The Romans stored their wine in the upper part of the house,—thus Horace says,—

" Descende Corvino jubente."—*Ode* xxi, *book* 3.

The object of such an arrangement was that the wine might ripen sooner by the heat and smoke, for the fires were made in the middle of their rooms with an outlet above for the smoke, which being driven upwards was collected in the upper apartment. Horace, referring to this practice, speaks of the smoke rolling to the top of the house :—

" Rotantes vertice fumum."—*Ode* xi, *book* 4.

We find Martial complaining of the wine being smoky, from the *amphora* not being hermetically closed, or *pitched*, as was their practice. Columella, in his work on Agriculture, gives the following directions for storing away the wine :—

" Apothecæ recte superponentur his locis unde plerumque fumus exoritur, quoniam vina celerius veterascunt quæ fumi quodam tenore præcocem maturitalem trahant."

*Book* i, *c.* 6.

WINE CART, and manner of filling the Amphora.

## CHAPTER II.

### Early History of the Vine.

" Next, ripe in yellow gold, a vineyard shines,
Bent with the ponderous harvest of its vines:
To this, one path-way gently winding leads,
Where march a train with baskets on their heads,
(Fair maids and blooming youths) that smiling bear
The purple product of th' autumnal year."

*' Iliad,'* book xviii—651.

IN treating of the history and management of wines, it would appear but natural that we should, in the first place, refer to the grape from which the wine is produced. The early history of the vine *(vitis vinifera)* is involved in considerable obscurity, for the oldest profane writers that mention it ascribe to it a fabulous origin. The tradition of the ancient Egyptians informs us that Osiris first paid attention to the vine, and instructed others in planting and using it. The inhabitants of Africa ascribe the cul-

tivation of the vine, and the art of making
wine from the fermented juice of the grape,
to the ancient Bacchus. The Bible informs
us that " Noah began to be a husbandman,
and planted a vineyard; " and we learn
from the same sacred authority, that the
spies whom Moses sent into Canaan, to
examine the land, went forth "at the time
of the first ripe grapes; " and a proof of
their estimation of the quality and plen-
teousness of the fruit contained in the
promised land, is exhibited by the fact of
their having cut at the brook of Eschol* a
cluster of grapes, which two of them bore
between them on a staff to the camp.
From the best authorities we can collect,
there remains no doubt as to the vine
being a native of Greece, of Turkey in
Asia, and of Persia. Dr. Sibthorp found
it abundant in a wild state throughout
the Morea; Pallas met with it growing
naturally near the Caspian and Black Seas;
Olivier saw it in many parts of the moun-

---

\* *Numbers,* xiii, 23.

tains of Koordistan; Michaux found it also
in the woods of Mazanderan; and on the
opposite side of Persia, a peculiar stoneless
variety, the *kismish*, is in all probability a
native of that part of the country lying on
the Persian Gulf.    Still further east, on
the northern shores of the Arabian Sea,
it has been found in Beloochistan.    It
grows, in company with the olive and fig,
along the bases of the Paropamisan mountains, extending to Caubulistan, where, with
the apricot and peach, it seems as perfectly
indigenous as in Anatolia and Karamania,
and in these it grows wild in the hearts
of the forests.    Baron Humboldt speaks
of it as growing wild on the banks of the
Caspian Sea, in Armenia, and Georgia.
Mr. Hawkins also bears testimony to its
being plentifully met with in a wild state
on the banks of the rivers of Greece.    In
Armenia it is known to abound; and as
the patriarch Noah planted a vineyard, it
may be inferred that this took place not
far from Mount Ararat, and that he found
the plants, of course indigenous, at no great

distance. In Syria the grape succeeds so well, that it has been by some considered its native country; and in no district have grapes been produced equal to those of Syria, as regards the size of the berries and extraordinary weight of the bunches, for at Damascus bunches are often found to weigh each from twenty to thirty pounds. Strabo relates that in Margiana bunches were met with two cubits (or a yard) long. Dr. Sickler, regarding the plant as of Persian origin, has given a learned and curious account of its migration thence to Egypt, Greece, and Sicily. From Sicily it is said to have been brought to Italy, Spain, and France. The Phocians are supposed to have carried it to the south of France, and the Romans to have planted it on the banks of the Rhine. Its progress through the remainder of southern Europe would be coeval with the extending influence of civilization.

# CHAPTER III.

### Vineyards in this Country.

*" Why weeps the muse for England ? what appears*
*In England's case, to move the muse to tears ?*
*Can nature add a charm, or art confer*
*A new-found luxury not seen in her ?"*—Cowper.

HE vine is said to have been introduced into England by the Romans ; and vineyards are mentioned in the earliest Saxon charters, as well as gardens and orchards.

Bede, writing in 731, alludes to vineyards being in existence at that time. Domesday Book also speaks of vineyards in several counties. William of Malmesbury, in his work, 'De Pontificibus,' written in 1123, informs us that the vale of Gloucester used to produce as good wine as many of the provinces of France. From the date of the Conquest, vineyards appear to have been attached to all the abbies and monastic institutions in the southern and western parts of the island. But about the time of the Reformation, when the ecclesiastical gardens were either neglected or destroyed, ale, which had been known in England for many centuries, seems to have superseded the use of wine as a general beverage. Stow, referring to the time of Richard II, tells us that "in many parts of England they grew vines and made wine; and such was the abundance of grapes in Windsor Park, that the king sold and made money by them." In the 'Museum Rusticum,' (i-185) it is stated that a vineyard flourished during the last century at Arundel Castle, in Sussex, and of its produce, there are reported to have been in 1763 in the Duke of Norfolk's cellars sixty pipes of wine resembling Burgundy. Hales, in his 'Practical Husbandry' (1727), says that he had drunk wine with Dr. Shaw, made by the latter from a small vineyard at Kensington, which he asserted was equal in quality to some of the higher wines of France. During the last century, the Hon. Charles Hamilton made some wine resembling champagne, from the produce of a vineyard near Cobham, in Surrey, situated on the southern slope of a hill, and which was planted with the species known as the Auvernat grape.

Although, there can be no doubt, as Professor Martyn observes, that "vineyards would succeed in the southern and western parts of England in proper soils, and produce wine equal to much that is imported from abroad;" yet, in a national point of view, we may conclude with Mr. Loudon, that "the culture of the vine as a branch of rural economy, would not be a profitable concern here, on the broad general principle, that it cannot be worth while to grow any thing at home, which we can get cheaper from abroad."

# CHAPTER IV.

## CLIMATES SUITABLE TO THE VINE.

" By Nature's all-refining hand prepar'd ;
Of temper'd sun, and water, earth and air,
In ever-changing composition mixed."
THOMSON. ' *The Seasons.*'

THE vine only thrives in particular climates, where the autumns are not excessively hot, nor the springs subject to late frosts. It has been observed in France, that the line which marks the northern boundary of the vineyards is not parallel to any circle of latitude; but that it lies obliquely, advancing more to the north on the eastern boundary of the country than on the western. It seems to depend more on the nature of the climate in spring and autumn, than in summer and winter. A hard frost at the time the sap is quiescent has no bad effect on the vine, but rather the contrary ; while a late frost in spring disappoints all the hopes of the vine-grower. In very cold regions the vine refuses to grow, and within 25° or even 30° of the equator it seldom flourishes so as to produce good fruit. Barton says,—" The cultivation of the vine succeeds only in those climates where the annual mean temperature is between 50° and 63°; or the mean temperature may be even as low as 48°, provided the summer heat rises to 68°. In the Old World these conditions are found to exist as far north as latitude 50°; in the New World not beyond latitude 40°. In both hemispheres the profitable culture of this plant ceases within 30° of the equator, unless in elevated situations, or in islands, such as Teneriffe, where the intensity of the heat is moderated by the atmosphere of the sea. Thus the region of vineyards occupies a band of about 20° in breadth in the Old World, and not more than half that breadth in America. In the southern hemisphere, the Cape of Good Hope just falls within the latitude adapted to the grape."

There are about twenty-one species of

vines, which are subdivided into innumerable varieties. The French government,
being desirous of bringing the cultivation
of the plant to the highest degree of perfection, a few years ago formed a nursery at
the Luxembourg, which was placed under
the superintendence of a scientific man, who
collected no less than 1400 varieties, and
he was then far from possessing all those
that were known in France; so much had
the various sorts been increased by the
influence of soil, climate, and culture.

## CHAPTER V.

.

------

### Culture of the Vine.

" I teach thee next the diff'ring soils to know,
The light for vines, the heavier for the plough."
*Georgics*, ii, 309.

------

T may be interesting to know how
the vine is cultivated in the countries which produce good wine ; of which
France is one of the principal, and nearest
in climate to England.   The vine grows
best in a soil where few other shrubs or
plants would thrive, and it seems a wise
distribution of Providence, that generally
where there is the best soil for wine, there
it is the worst for wheat, and *vice-versa.*

The vine delights in a deep loose rocky
soil, where its roots can penetrate deep into
fissures, so as to ensure a supply of moisture when the surface is scorched by the
sun's rays.   Miller, in the ' Gardener's

Dictionary,' says,—" The best soil for a vineyard in England is a light sandy loam, about a foot and a half, but not more than two feet, deep above the gravel or chalk, either of which bottoms are good."

On the steep slopes of hills towards the south, and sheltered from the north-east, the grapes attain the highest perfection, and the vintage is most certain. So great an influence has a favourable position, that in the same vineyard a very considerable difference exists between the wine made from one part and that made from another, merely because there is a turn round the hill, and the aspect varies a few degrees. A change of soil produces a similar effect. The famous Rhine wine, *Johannisberg*, when made with the grapes which grow near the castle, is worth twice as much as that made a few hundred yards further off, owing to difference both in soil and aspect. The *Clos de Vougeôt* which produces the finest burgundy, is confined to a few acres; outside the walls the wine is but of moderate quality. This perfection results almost entirely

from natural causes, and is not brought about
by manuring or other artificial means; for
in the best vineyards no manures are used
except those of a vegetable nature, such as
the leaves and tendrils of the plant, the
residue of the grape when pressed, or the
leaves of other trees; and these are generally formed into a compost with earth.
Indeed we are told that a celebrated vineyard, many years ago in the possession of
General Kellerman, was very much reduced
in value from being manured, and that it
was several years before it regained its
former reputation.

Artificial heat was not applied to the
production of grapes before the beginning
of the last century. The first instance we
find occurs in Lawrence's 'Fruit Calendar,'
1718, wherein it is stated that at the Duke of
Rutland's, at Belvoir Castle, fires were constantly kept up, from Lady-day to Michael-
mas, behind the slope-walls on which the
plants were trained. The art of forcing
has most probably gradually diverted the
attention of gardeners from the cultivation

of the vine in the open air. Mr. Loudon
says, that "no kitchen garden worth notice
is now without a vinery; the fruit is produced in some vineries in every month of
the year; and in the London market is to
be had in the highest degree of perfection
from March to January."

The species of grape distinguished above
all others for its size is a thick-skinned
white variety, called the Syrian, and which,
preserving its characteristic in this respect,
has been more or less grown in this country.
A bunch of this description of grape was
gathered in 1781, at Welbeck, near Work-
sop, the seat of the Duke of Portland,
weighing 19½ pounds; it was upwards of
21 inches in length, and 19 inches across
the shoulders. The well-known vine at
Hampton Court Palace, of the red Ham-
burgh species, has produced 2200 bunches,
averaging one pound each, or in all nearly
a ton. Another plant at Valentine House,
in Essex, has yielded 2000 bunches of
nearly the same average weight. In 1789,
a vine was growing at Northallerton, which

covered a space of 137 square yards; and
another is mentioned at Ilford, in Essex, of
which the stem was 19 inches in girth, and
the branches 200 feet long.

All authorities concur in stating that the
vine attains an age equal, at least, to that
of the oak; a vineyard a hundred years
old being considered young. Pliny speaks
of a vine which had existed six hundred
years; and Bosc says, there are vines in
Burgundy upwards of four hundred years
of age.

# CHAPTER VI.

### VINEYARDS OF FRANCE AND ITALY.

" Sweet is the vintage, when the showering grapes
   In Bacchanal profusion reel to earth
  Purple and gushing."
          BYRON. *'Don Juan,'* *canto* i, *st.* 124.

UR imagination is apt to be wonderfully taken with the idea of a country covered with vines, and glowing with their luscious fruit, and it is ten to one if the "vineclad hills" do not present the most prominent feature in the idea generally formed by any one who has not visited France. The vine, however, is not an object of such striking beauty in France as is generally supposed; and indeed it cannot bear comparison with the finest of our hop-gardens of Kent. The common way of planting the vine is to fix down a stake about four feet high to each vine, and this method of low training, which is the only one suitable to the climate, gives the plant a stunted

appearance. Before the foliage has dis-
played itself, nothing but a field of stakes
is visible. "At this time," says Mr. Cobbett,
in his ' Tour in France,' " the vine is ugly.
It looks like currant bushes, or any low
and leafless sort of shrub." He further
observes that " the idea of a whole country
covered over with black and white grapes
is a rich one; and it is but natural we
should suppose the makers of Burgundy
rich in proportion to the richness of the
luxury they produce; but vines are subjected
to so many chances, that there is not a
poorer country than that which is covered
with them."

It is the vineyards of Italy which are
really beautiful, and which, rather than
those of France, are worthy of being pictured in the choicest colours. The last
writer whom we have quoted says,—" I
cannot help envying the Italians one charm
that their country possesses—I mean her
vines. Here the fields have rows of trees
planted round them ; and the trunks and
branches of these trees are the supporters

of the vine,—the greatest embellishment
that a country can possibly have. The
vine is not at all the same thing here that
it is in France. The French cut it down
nearly as we cut our currant bushes, check
its vigorous and aspiring shoots, and confine
them to the height of a mere stake. But
here each individual tree, or row of trees,
with the vines clambering up and hanging
from the branches is an object of admiration
in itself. The poplar and the common
maple are the trees most commonly used
to train the vine to. These trees do not so
much overshadow it as most other trees
would, as they are not allowed to grow to
their full height. In training the vine, a
main object seems to be that of directing
the shoots downwards; and this is done in
order to make them bear more fruit. The
yearling shoots that are to bear fruit in the
following summer are brought together in
twos; each two are twisted round and
round one another, cut off at a certain
distance and tied together with a twig of
osier. The shoots thus managed hang

over the branches of the tree with their
ends towards the ground. Some of them
are bent outwards, in the form of a bow,
the ends being tied in to the tree, or to the
main stem of the vine. Others are led
away from the tree, and have their ends
tied to the tops of high stakes, at four or
five yards off. Great taste is shewn by
these people in this matter. They give it
all the variety that such a thing can admit
of. One of the forms is particularly elegant;
—two couples of twined shoots are brought
to meet each other half way between two
trees, then tied together, and their extremities bent right and left, and tied again in
such a way as to make a festoon. In summer and autumn the broad leaves, tendrils,
and clusters of grapes are beautiful." The
same writer, describing the road between
Rome and Naples, states that "within a
few miles of Naples the vines are trained
to elms or poplars, generally the latter.
These trees grow to their natural height,
the side branches being lopped away just
enough to let in the sunshine between them.

Only think of fifty or sixty acres of land
in this way; high poplars standing in rows
with wide intervals; vines clambering up
every tree, their long shoots led from the
branches of one tree to those of another,
crossing in all directions, some of them
hanging down towards the ground! Luxuriant crops* grow under the trees; capital
wheat, now all in ear, and turning yellow;
fine Indian corn, planted in drills from two
to three feet apart, besides oats and beans,
and other things. Thus is the land cultivated for miles before you come to Naples."

It would be difficult to form an idea of
the beauty of the vineyards of this bright
sunny clime, and of the joyousness attendant
on the gathering in of the fruit. Mr.
Beckford, who visited Italy nearly eighty
years ago, describes in his 'Sketches' the
luxuriant manner in which the vine grows
near Lucca:—" Mounting our horses, we
wound among sunny vales and enclosures

---

* " Fields waving high with heavy crops are seen,
And vines that flourish in eternal green."
*Odyssey, book* ix—153.

with myrtle hedges, till we came to a rapid
steep.  We felt the heat most powerfully
in ascending it, and were glad to take
refuge under a continued bower of vines,
which runs for miles along its summit.
These arbours afforded us both shade and
refreshment.  I fell upon the clusters which
formed our ceiling, like a native of the
north, unused to such luxuries; one of those
Goths Gray so poetically describes, who

" Scent the new fragrance of the breathing rose,
   And quaff the pendant vintage as it grows ! "

All who have travelled in Italy give a
glowing account of the beauty of the Italian
vineyards, and those who have witnessed
the bright and unclouded scene of universal
mirth and rejoicing at the time of collecting
the bountiful and luxuriant produce, describe it in language the most picturesque,—
nay almost extravagant.  Mr. Forsyth, in
his ' Excursion in Italy,' says, " The vintage
was now in full glow.  Men, women,
children, asses, all were variously engaged
in the work.  I remarked in the scene a

prodigality and negligence which I never saw in France. The grapes dropped un-heeded from the panniers, and hundreds were left unclipped on the vine." One of our favourite poets thus describes it:—

> " The vines in light festoons
> From tree to tree, the trees in avenues,
> And every avenue a covered walk,
> Hung black with clusters. 'Tis enough to make
> The sad man merry, the benevolent one
> Melt into tears, so general is the joy."
>
> ROGERS' *' Italy.'*

The soil is so fertile that, to borrow Douglas Jerrold's witty conceit, if you tickle it with a hoe it smiles with a flower; but it too frequently happens that where Nature is most bountiful, man becomes more remiss and unmindful of her gifts, and fails to improve the benefits lavished upon him. The vines are frequently left to trail un-heeded round each other, occasionally on the ground, and no pains are taken to prune them so as to improve the growth and quality of the grape. In spite, however, of every error in culture, the crop in ordi-nary seasons is immense, and the great superiority of climate might with moderate attention ensure a high rank to the wines of Italy,

> " Were they content to prune the lavish vine
> Of straggling branches, and improve the wine."
>
> DRYDEN.

But from the slovenly indolence of the natives, and total disregard of any thing like a system for making the most of their produce, the quality of the wine is almost always in the inverse ratio of profuse production. A writer, in a recent and well-written volume, remarks with truth,—" If Italy could produce superlative wines in the time of Augustus, why not now, with an undiminished sun and unimpaired soil, and every modern appliance to boot ? Verily, to this end freedom alone is wanting, —freedom of thought and freedom of action, —for the dawn of a brighter future is already responding to the aspirations of an ardent and intellectual people."

# CHAPTER VII.

———

## WINE CHEMICALLY CONSIDERED.

" Happy the man, who studying Nature's laws,
Through known effects can trace the secret cause."
*Georgics*, ii, 698.

———

HE term wine is more strictly and specially applied to express the fermented juice of the *grape*, although it is generally used to denote that of *any* sub-acid fruit. The presence of *tartar* is perhaps the circumstance by which the grape is most strongly distinguished from all the other sub-acid fruits that have been applied to the purpose of wine making. The juice of the grape, moreover, contains within itself all the principles essential to vinification, in such a proportion and state of balance as to enable it at once to undergo a regular and complete fermentation; whereas the juices of other fruits require artificial additions for this purpose; and the scientific application and due adjustment of these means constitute the art of wine-making. For a more detailed account of this process, the reader is referred to an interesting work by Dr. M'Culloch, entitled 'Remarks on the Art of making Wine, with suggestions for the application of its principles to the improvement of Domestic Wines.'

In the adulteration of Wines, three principal objects are attempted, viz.—1. *To give them strength*, which is effected by adding any ardent spirit; but the wine is slowly decomposed by it. 2. *To perfect or change their colour.* It was formerly a common practice to change *white* wines, when they had become brown or rough, into *red* wines, by means of sloes, or other colouring matter. 3. *To lessen or remove their acidity.* The ancients, it would appear, were acquainted with this property in lead, for according to Pliny, the Greeks and Romans improved the quality of their wines by immersing a plate of lead in them. But the object more to be desired by the use of lead was doubtless to lessen the acidity which belonged to the wine, or which it had acquired by keeping. We are disposed, however, to regard the practice as one highly reprehensible and productive of mischievous results; and can scarcely imagine that any conscientious dealer would resort to so dangerous an expedient. Dr. M'Culloch considered that little harm could ensue, since the compounds formed by the mixture of the metal with the tartaric and malic acids are insoluble. Although literally true, this must only be taken for what it is worth, since by any slight addition of acid, the blending with unsound wine for instance, or even by a reaction within the wine itself, the lead would be liberated, and a *soluble* triple salt, *aceto-tartrate of lead* would be produced. The presence of lead, however, may be easily detected by the test invented by Dr. Hahnemann. Expose equal parts of sulphur and prepared chalk to a white heat for fifteen minutes, and when cold add an equal quantity of cream of tartar; these are to be put into a strong bottle with

D

common water and boiled for an hour; and
the solution is afterwards to be decanted
into ounce phials, adding twenty drops of
muriatic acid to each. This liquor will
precipitate the least quantity of lead from
wines in a black sediment. As iron might
be accidentally contained in the wine, the
muriatic acid is added to prevent its pre-
cipitation. Or we would suggest a more
simple test — a solution of prussiate of
potass, a few drops of which will throw
down a white precipitate if lead be present;
or again, sulphuretted-hydrogen will dis-
engage the lead in the form of a dark
brown sediment.

Mr. Brande has constructed a table, a
copy of which is annexed, exhibiting the
proportions of *combined* alcohol which exist
in the several kinds of wine ; and the fact
of the difference of effect, produced by the
same bulk of vinous spirit, when presented
to the stomach in different states of combi-
nation, adds another striking and instructive
illustration of the extraordinary powers of
chemical arrangement in modifying the

activity of substances upon the living system. We are now referring to wine in its *pure* state, but it is necessary to observe, that inferior wines are frequently rendered marketable in this country by the addition of brandy, and must consequently contain *uncombined* alcohol; at the period of this admixture a renewed fermentation is produced, which assimilates and combines a certain portion of the foreign spirit with the wine. This method of fortifying wines has been practised for many years, the Excise authorities permitting the use of brandy to the extent of ten per cent. for that purpose; and the process is absolutely necessary as regards the lower classed wines. The manipulation is technically termed *fretting-in.* The free alcohol may, however, be separated by saturating the vinous fluid with *sub-carbonate of potass*, while the combined portion will remain undisturbed. In ascertaining the genuineness of a wine, this circumstance ought always to constitute a leading feature in the enquiry; and the tables of Mr. Brande would have been greatly enhanced in practical value, had the relative proportions of *uncombined* spirit been appreciated in his experiments, since it is to *this*, and not to the *combined* alcohol, that any injurious effects attending the use of wine are to be attributed.

The constituents of wine, according to Gmelin (*'Handbuch d Chemie,'* b. ii, p. 1255), are as follows :—*Alcohol, an odorous principle* (volatile oil ?), *blue colouring matter of the husk* (in red wine), *tannin, bitter extractive, sugar* (especially in the sweet wines), *gum, yeast, acetic acid* (from the commencement of the acetous fermentation), *malic acid, tartaric acid, bitartrate of potass, bitartrate of lime, sulphates* and *chlorides, phosphate of lime, carbonic acid* (especially in the effervescing wines), and *water.* To these may be added *paratartaric* or *racemic acid.* The tartar and dregs of wine are not lost, being employed in commerce ; the tartar is used in medicine and dyeing ; and the dregs are dried, and serve the hatter in the dyeing and fabrication of hats.

*Mr. Brande's Table of the proportion of Alcohol (sp. gr. 0·825 at 60° F.), by measure, contained in 100 parts of Wine.*

| No. | Wine | Value | No. | Wine | Value |
|---|---|---|---|---|---|
| 1 | Lissa | 25·41 | 21 | White Hermitage | 17·43 |
| 2 | Raisin | 25·12 | 22 | Roussillon | 18·13 |
| 3 | Marsala | 25·09 | 23 | Claret | 15·10 |
| 4 | Port | 22·96 | 24 | Zante | 17·05 |
| 5 | Madeira | 22·27 | 25 | Malmsey Madeira | 16·40 |
| 6 | Sherry | 19·17 | 26 | Lunel | 15·52 |
| 7 | Teneriffe | 19·79 | 27 | Shiraz | 15·52 |
| 8 | Colares | 19·75 | 28 | Syracuse | 15·28 |
| 9 | Lachrymæ Christi | 19·70 | 29 | Sauterne | 14·22 |
| 10 | Constantia, white | 19·75 | 30 | Burgundy | 14·57 |
| 11 | Constantia, red | 18·92 | 31 | Hock | 12·08 |
| 12 | Lisbon | 18·94 | 32 | Nice | 14·63 |
| 13 | Malaga | 18·94 | 33 | Barsac | 13·86 |
| 14 | Bucellas | 18·49 | 34 | Tent | 13·30 |
| 15 | Red Madeira | 20·35 | 35 | Champagne | 12·61 |
| 16 | Cape Muschat | 18·25 | 36 | Red Hermitage | 12·32 |
| 17 | Cape Madeira | 20·51 | 37 | Vin de Grave | 13·94 |
| 18 | Calcavella | 18·65 | 38 | Frontignac | 12·79 |
| 19 | Vidonia | 19·25 | 39 | Côté Rôtie | 12·32 |
| 20 | Alba Flora | 17·26 | 40 | Tokay | 9·88 |

# CHAPTER VIII.

WINE CONSIDERED IN RELATION TO HEALTH
AND DISEASE.

" The weary find new strength in generous wine."
　　　　　　HOMER. '*Iliad,*' *book* vi, 261.

" Three cups of wine a prudent man may take ;
　The first of them for constitution sake ;
　The second to the girl he loves the best ;
　The third and last to lull him to his rest—
　Then home to bed."
　　　　*Translated from* ' *Deipnosophistæ, or Banquet of the*
*Learned,*' *a Greek work by Athenæus (3rd century) book* ii. *c.* 3.

N a dietetical point of view wine is
useful or prejudicial, in proportion
as the fermentation is more or less perfect.
In wines containing malic acid, when the
fermentation has been imperfect, the fermen-
tative state of the liquor is recommenced in
the stomach, and carbonic and other gases
are evolved, which, distending that organ,
oppress the individual ; and, if he be dys-
peptic, produce depression of spirits and
all the horrors of hypochondriacism. But

when met with pure in quality and of
proper age, the temperate use of wine may
be said to promote digestion, exhilarate the
spirits, sharpen the wit, and call into action
all the intellectual powers. Plato, while he
would restrict the use of wine, and severely
censure its excess, maintains with more
than his usual persuasive power, that "nothing more excellent than the juice of the
grape was ever granted by God to man."
In sacred writ, Paul exhorts Timothy to
"drink no longer water, but use a little
wine for thy stomach's sake and thine often
infirmities."—*Timothy* v, 23. Burton, in
his 'Anatomy of Melancholy,' quaintly observes, that "a cup of generous wine to
those whose minds are still and motionless,
is, in my opinion, excellent physic." Dr.
Sandford, in his 'Remarks on the Medi-
cinal Effects of Wines and Spirits,' says,
"Wine is undoubtedly one of those real
blessings with which a kind Providence has
favoured us ; and its true uses and effects
have been long known and considered by
medical writers of very high eminence and

authority. The power of making 'glad the heart of man,' must therefore, by every person of discernment and observation, be allowed to have been justly ascribed to it by David, and within the limits prescribed I would urge its use to be strictly confined." Dr. Holdsworth says, "*Pure* wine upon a *healthy* stomach is grateful and precious as the light of truth and the exercise of discretion to a sound and well-regulated mind." Dr. M'Culloch writes, "Whilst it is well known that diseases of the liver are the most common, as well as the most formidable of those produced by the use of *ardent* spirits, it is equally certain that no such disorders follow even the intemperate use of *pure* wine, however long indulged in." Dr. Brinton, in his work 'On Food,' remarks, "From good wine, in moderate quantity, there is no reaction whatever." Dr. Pereira says, "The most perfect health is compatible with the moderate enjoyment of wine, and many individuals who attain a good long age, have for a length of time been in the habit of using wine daily, and are likely to suffer if deprived of their natural stimulus." Dr. Paris writes, "There exists no evidence to prove that a temperate use of good wine, when taken at seasonable hours, has ever proved injurious to healthy adults;" and this opinion can scarcely be opposed, since he has so qualified the sentence, that in any case where ill effects might appear to result from the use of wine by adults, they may safely be ascribed to the non-fulfilment of some of the conditions here mentioned,—viz. the *temperate* use of wine,—the *goodness* of the liquor,— the *seasonable* time of taking it,—or the *health* of the individual.

Champagne and other effervescent wines are frequently recommended by the faculty in cases of great prostration of strength. Stimulant, without being irritant, their restorative properties cannot be too highly prized, since by their use, the failing powers of nature are frequently so assisted as to bear up successfully against disease.

To attempt to give rules for the employment of wine, or to fix the kind proper for

different invalids, is impossible; the observation of Van Swieten being as applicable
to wine as to food : " To say what kind is
suitable, without knowing for whom, is as
absurd as to assert that the wind is favourable, without knowing to what port the ship
intends to sail." All invalids, and indeed
others, should avoid mixing wines; the
reason for this rule is obvious,—when two
wines are mixed more or less fermentation
occurs, which a weak stomach is unable to
control. The question whether wine should
be taken at all by those in health need not
be discussed here. The universal consent
of mankind has settled the question, and
none but one-sided individuals would aim
at depriving their fellow-creatures of one
of the best gifts of Providence—which
lightens the toil of civilized life and
heightens its enjoyments, because a few
are to be found who may occasionally
abuse it.

An amusing story is told of the famed
Dr. Busby, Head Master of Westminster
School, that on a certain occasion he in-

vited the boys to partake of a glass of wine. Being noted for his parsimonious habits, this unwonted liberality excited some little surprise, which the Doctor observing, re-marked " Aliquantum vini ingenium acuit" (a little wine sharpens the wit). One boy, more forward than the rest, having tossed off his wine, and holding out the empty glass, exclaimed, " Plus vini, plus ingenii" (the more wine, the more wit). " No, no," says the Doctor, "although you argue on *mathematical principles*, no more wine."

# CHAPTER IX.

## Authors who have written on the subject of Wine.

*" In jovial songs they praise the god of wine."*
*Georgics* ij, 535.

HE vine has supplied to writers a subject as fertile as the plant itself, and wine has been a favourite theme with poets of all ages from the days of Homer to the present time. Speaking of a wine of which neither the name nor species has been handed down to us, the father of poetry describes it as " rich, unadulterate, and fit drink for the gods." Anacreon, who lived nearly 600 years B.C., sings its praises, and calls the juice of the grape " ambrosial." Phocylides, a Greek philosopher, born 535 B.C., writing on the subject, directs that the wine should freely circulate round the board and be enlivened by cheerful conversation.* Mago, a Carthaginian, born 550 years before the Christian era, wrote twenty-eight books on Husbandry, and gave minute directions for gathering and pressing the grape. That the same rules prevailed about 600 years afterwards, we have the testimony of Columella, a writer on Agriculture, born about the beginning of the Christian era, who says that "Mago gives similar directions for making the best sort of wine as I have done." Democritus, born 460 B.C., Plato, born 429 B.C., and Aristotle, born 384 B.C., have also contributed to the subject. Of the medical authorities of those days, Hippocrates, born 460 B.C., and Galen, born A.D. 131, speak highly of wine as a remedial

---

* Professor Wilson adopted this Greek couplet as the motto of the celebrated ' Noctes Ambrosianæ,' published in ' Blackwood's Magazine,' and thus refers to it :—

" This is a distich by wise old Phocylides,
An ancient who wrote crabbed Greek in no silly days :
Meaning, ' 'tis right for good wine-bibbing people
Not to let the glass pass the board like a cripple,
But gaily to talk whilst they're quaffing their tipple.' "

agent. The former gives a lengthened
description of the Greek wines, and points
out in what diseases, and in what quantities
they are to be taken. Cato, in his work,
' De Re Rustica,' written about 185 B.C.,
speaks of the culture of the vine, and
referring to the manufacture of wine, recommends that " the sea water should be
taken up to the mountains, a great distance
from the land, and there kept for some time
previous to being used." It is traditionally
stated that this practice had its origin in
the following circumstance. A slave, who
had stolen some wine, to escape detection,
supplied the deficiency by filling up the
vessel with sea water. On examining the
stock, the quantity was found to be so
much in excess, that the offender, on being
questioned, confessed his guilt; but the
quality of the wine was considered so
much improved by the addition, that the
use of salt water was generally adopted.
For this purpose, the water was directed
to be taken up as far as possible from the
shore, in a calm clear day, and boiled down

to about a third part before it was added to the wine. Varro, who likewise wrote on the subject, and under the same title also, about 120 years afterwards, treats of the method of planting vineyards. Although Varro wrote this work at the age of eighty, it may be said to be the best of the Roman treatises on Agriculture that have been handed down to us. Cicero, who was born 106 years B.C., referring to wines, says, " One of the most lucrative of commercial transactions among the Gauls was the exportation of their wine to Italy." Virgil and Tibullus in their day wrote on wines ; the former in praising the *vinum Rhæticum*, says, " it must, nevertheless, yield the palm to the *Falernian.*" The Odes of Horace abound in allusions to the grape and its juicy product, and shew the high estimation in which wine was regarded by the ancient Romans. His cotemporaries, Martial and Juvenal, have also written on the subject. Some years later, Ovid, who was born 43 B.C., sung the praises of wine. Zeno, also, wrote a work on wines, probably

about the year B.C. 464, and extols their
exhilarating effects.

"Zeno, Plato, Aristotle,
All were lovers of the bottle."

This distich, however, must be received
*cum grano salis*, at least as regards Plato,
for although he has referred to the beneficial
use of wine, he has laid down most stringent
rules against it being taken in excess. Pliny,
born A.D. 23, carefully collected all that had
been written before his time on the subject
of the vine. He describes the various
species of the *vitis*, and the mode of
making wine, enumerating at the same
time the principal wines of Asia, Greece,
and Italy. Erasmus, born 1467, extols the
use of wine; and we are told that being
tormented with nephritic pains, he took to
drinking Burgundy, and soon became perfectly restored. "Happy province!" he
exclaims, "well may Burgundy be called
the mother of man, suckling him with such
milk!" Patin, writing in 1669, referring
also to the wines of France, says, "Long

live the bread of Gonesse, with the good wines of Paris, Burgundy, and Champagne." Paumier, a Norman physician, wrote a 'Treatise on Wine,' in 1588. Lord Bacon, in the days of Queen Elizabeth, did not disdain to give his attention to the subject. Andrea Baccius, physician to Sextus the Fifth, has given us a good history of wine in that rare and curious book, 'De Naturali Vinorum Historia,' published in 1596. About a century ago, Sir Edward Barry, then a physician at Bath, and afterwards state physician to the Viceroy of Ireland, published his 'Observations, Historical, Critical, and Medical, on the Wines of the Ancients; and on the Analogy between them and Modern Wines.' In consequence of the interest excited by the topic, the work acquired a certain amount of repute at the time, but it is not held in much estimation at the present day. The late Dr. Henderson, in 1824, published his 'History of Ancient and Modern Wines,' which contains much interesting and useful information. But perhaps the best and

most comprehensive work on the subject is
that by Mr. Cyrus Redding, called a ' History and Description of Modern Wines,'
published in 1836. Dr. M'Culloch has
also written a useful volume ' On Wines.'
Busby's ' Visit to the Vineyards of Spain
and France' contains an interesting account
of the various modes of culture of the vine
peculiar to different countries, as well as
much information on the subject of wine.
Chaptal, a French chemist, gives a good
description of the French wines in his
' Traité théorique et pratique sur la Culture
de la Vigne,' published in 1801. Jullien's
work ' Topographie de tous les Vignobles
connus' (1822) is an authority frequently
referred to; but perhaps the best work on
the wines of France is Paguierre's ' Wines
of Bordeaux' (1828). The volume published by Mr. Forrester on ' Port and the
wines of Portugal' (1854) is a work highly
esteemed, and for fulness of detail, at least
as regards port wine, has seldom been surpassed. There is also ' Wine and Wine
Countries,' by Mr. Tovey of Bristol (1862).

Two other works have recently been published on the subject, ' Wine, the Vine, and
the Cellar,' by Mr. T. G. Shaw; and ' The
Vine and its Fruit,' by Mr. J. L. Denman;
both of which are exceedingly well got up,
and contain much valuable information.
Of the German authors who have contributed to the subject, we may mention
Bronner's 'Wienbau in Frankreich,' ' Weinbau in Süd-Deutschland,' and his ' Die
Teutschen Schaumereine;' Schams' ' Un-
garns Weinbau;' and Graff's ' Der Mosel-
wein als Getrank und Heilmittel.'

# CHAPTER X.

GENERAL ARRANGEMENT AND CLASSIFI-
CATION OF WINES.

" This truth premised was needful as a text
To win due credence to what follows next."
COWPER.

WINES admit of being arranged under
four classes.

1. SWEET WINES,—which contain the
greatest proportion of extractive and saccharine matter, and generally the least
ardent spirit, though this is often rather
disguised than absent; as in these wines a
proportion of sugar has remained unchanged
during the process of vinification, they
must be considered as the results of an
imperfect fermentation, and are in fact
mixtures of wine and sugar; accordingly,
whatever arrests the progress of fermen-

tation, must have a tendency to produce a sweet wine; thus boiling the *must* or drying the fruit will, by partially separating the natural leaven and dissipating the water, occasion such a result as is exemplified by the manufacture of the wines of Cyprus, the *vino cotto* of the Italians, and the *vinum coctum* of the ancients, by that of *Frontignac*, the rich and luscious wines of *Canary*, the celebrated *Tokay*, *Vino Tento* (Tent of Hungary), the Italian *Montefiascone*, the Persian *Schiraz*, the *Malmsey wines of Candia, Chio, Lesbos, and Tenedos*, and those of the other islands of the Archipelago.

2. SPARKLING or EFFERVESCING WINES, as Champagne, &c. are indebted for their characteristic properties to the presence of carbonic acid; they rapidly intoxicate, in consequence of the alcohol, which is suspended in, or combined with the gas, being thus applied in a sudden and very divided state to a large extent of nervous surface; for the same reason, their effects are as transient as they are sudden.

3. DRY AND LIGHT. These are exemplified by the more esteemed German wines,

as *Hock, Rhenish, Maine, Moselle, Necker,*
and *Elsass,* and those highly flavoured
wines *Burgundy, Claret, Hermitage,* &c.
They contain a very inconsiderable degree
of ardent spirit, and combine with it the
effect of an acid.

4. DRY AND STRONG, as *Madeira, Port,
Sherry,* &c. Wines which contain a comparatively small quantity of spirit are termed
*light wines;* whilst those which have a
much larger quantity are denominated
*strong* or *generous wines.*

The wines of different countries are distinguished in commerce by various names.
The following is a list of the wines most
commonly met with, arranged according to
the countries producing them :—

1. FRENCH WINES.—*Champagne; Burgundy* (red and white); *Hermitage; Rous-
sillon; Frontignac; Claret* (the most esteemed being the produce of *Lafitte, Latour,
Château Margaux,* and *Haut Brion); Vin
de Grave; Sauterne;* and *Barsac.*

2. SPANISH WINES. — *Sherry* (Xeres);
*Tent* (Rota); *Mountain* (Malaga); *Benicarlo* (Alicant).

3. PORTUGAL WINES.—*Port* (Oporto) ; *Bucellas, Lisbon, Calcavella,* and *Colares* (Lisbon).

4. GERMAN WINES.—*Rhine and Moselle Wines.* The term *Hock* is usually applied to the first growths of the Rhine, whilst the term *Rhenish* commonly indicates an inferior Rhine wine.

5. HUNGARIAN WINES.—*Tokay,* &c.

6. ITALIAN AND SICILIAN WINES.— *Lachrymæ Christi ; Marsala ; Syracuse ; Lissa.*

7. GRECIAN AND IONIAN WINES.—*Candian* and *Cyprus* wines.

8. WINES OF MADEIRA AND THE CANARY ISLANDS.—*Madeira* and *Vidonia* (Teneriffe).

9. WINES OF THE CAPE OF GOOD HOPE. —*Cape Madeira ; Constantia* (red and white).

10. PERSIAN WINES.—*Shiraz.*

11. AUSTRIAN WINES.—*Vöslauer ; Goldeck ; Steinberg ;* &c.

12. ENGLISH WINES.—*Grape ; Raisin ; Currant ; Gooseberry ; Ginger ;* &c.

# CHAPTER XI.

---

## ON THE WINES OF FRANCE.

" Thus the wool of England used to be exchanged for the wines of France."
Adam Smith. '*Wealth of Nations,*' Book iii, *c.* 3.

" Benedetto
Quel Claretto !"—Francesco Redi.

" Que le Vieillard cherche un reste de vie
Dans le Bourdeaux qui réchauffe les sens,
Pour charmer ses banquets la Jeunesse n'envie
Que la Champagne aux flots resplendissants."
Amaury de Cazanove.

" A goblet of Burgundy fill, fill for me,
Give those who prefer it Champagne."
*Old Song.*

---

N taking a review of the wines of each particular country, it is but courteous as well as appropriate that we should commence with those of our nearest continental neighbour.

France is divided, for fiscal purposes,

into seventy-six wine districts, in the same way that England is sub-divided by the Board of Excise into districts termed " collections." The total superficies of France is not quite 53,000,000 hectares,* the uncultivated lands amounting to nearly one-eighth of the whole. More than one-thirtieth part of France, including the waste lands, is cultivated in vineyards; this is equivalent to about a seventh part of England. The *value* of the annual produce of the vineyards has been estimated at £28,040,000; and the *quantity* of wine produced in a year at 998,932,900 gallons, giving about 200 gallons per acre. The wine-growers are supposed to be about 1,800,000 in number.

The district in which the production of wine is carried on to the largest extent, and where the cultivation of the vine is most advanced, as well as the qualities of the wine itself of the highest order, is the department of the Gironde. The superficies of the Gironde is 1,200,000 hectares,

---

* The hectare is 2 acres 1⅞ rood English.

and the extent of vineyards is equal to
350,000 English acres.  The average produce of this district is about 60,000,000
gallons, five-eights of which are red, and
three-eights white wine.  In very favourable
years the quantity will amount to nearly
80,000,000 gallons.

The value of vineyard property varies
very much.  The Mouton estate, consisting
of 135 acres, was sold in 1830 at the rate
of £356 per acre; this is the highest price
ever paid.  The estate of Lafitte, consisting
of 262 acres, was sold in 1803 at the rate
£183 4s. per acre.  Both these estates are
situate in the Médoc district.  About 5154
acres of Médoc wine estates have been sold
in the present century; the average amount
obtained was £64 per acre.

The difference in the value of wine of
the same vineyard varies exceedingly from
one year to another, according to the season
being favourable or unfavourable.  The
produce of Château Lafitte, Château Latour,
and Château Margaux, which are the most
esteemed vineyards, has been as low as

£30 per hogshead* in a bad year. On the other hand it has, under different circumstances, been as high as £70.

The red wines from Bourdeaux, which pass under the name of *Claret* in England, come from several districts in the neighbourhood of that city. Those from the Médoc are of the highest quality, and include the celebrated vineyards Château Lafitte, Château Latour, and Château Margaux. After these come the growths of St. Emelion, in the arrondissement of Libourne, and are the growth of three communes. Next may be mentioned the Vins de Graves, so called from the gravelly nature of the soil; it is in this district that the Haut Brion is situated. The Graves wines grow upon 18 communes.

The Côtes wines derive the name from the vineyards being situate on the sides or slopes of the hills; and in point of situation they are highly favoured. They are the produce of 24 communes.

---

* A hogshead of French wine is 46 gallons.

On the shores of, and between the rivers
Dordogne and Garonne, are the Libournais,
Blayais, and Bourgais vineyards; these are
about the least valuable of the Bourdeaux
wines, and were formerly sold chiefly as
cargo wines for exportation to the colonies,
although they are frequently palmed off as
the produce of Médoc.  The wine of Rous-
sillon is largely used in blending with the
common wines of Bourdeaux to form an
article of Claret, yet even in its natural
state it has failed to impress us with any
favourable opinion as to its merits, and
although the wines of the Bourdelais are
familiarly known to the public under the
term Claret, yet there is but a comparatively
small quantity that would be recognized
either by the dealer or the grower as being
worthy of that distinctive appellation.  They
are classed by the *crus* or growth, according
to the quality.  Thus in Bourdeaux there
are four estates or growths classed as first
*crus* or growths ; eleven classed as second ;
fourteen classed as third ; eleven classed
as fourth ; and seventeen classed as fifth

growths; making altogether fifty-seven estates.

It is not an unusual occurrence for an agent to purchase the produce of a vine-yard before the grapes are gathered. It may not be uninteresting to know that a contract was signed in March of the present year, between M. le Vicomte Aguado, proprietor of the estate of Château Margaux, and three eminent London firms, by which the latter have secured the entire produce of this celebrated growth for a long term of years.

The best Clarets are those known as *Château Margaux, Lafitte, Latour, Haut Brion, Mouton, Leoville, Rauzan, St. Emelion,* &c.

The south-western part of the department of the Gironde, especially on the left bank of the Garonne, is mostly productive of white wines. It is there that the *Sauterne* wines are produced, as well as those of *Barsac* and *Graves*. The finest of the Sauterne wines is called *Château Yquem,* and is distinguished above all other sorts

for its fine delicate flavour and *bouquet.*
The *Barsac* and *Graves* white wines are
also of very good quality, but the other
growths do not require any particular notice.

The vineyards producing *Hermitage* are
situated upon the slopes of hills near the
town of Tain on the left bank of the
Rhòne, southward of Lyons. Mr. Cyrus
Redding gives the following singular account
of their origin:—" Tradition says, that an
inhabitant of the town of Condrieux determined to turn hermit, and established
his cell on an uncultivated hill near Tain.
He amused his leisure hours by breaking
the stones and rocks to pieces which surrounded his dwelling, and planting among
them some vine slips from Condrieux. They
succeeded to admiration. His example was
copied by others, and the sterile hill-side
was soon converted into a vineyard. The
good taste of the monks in wine has been
already remarked in other places. Thus
to the hypocrisy of the mortifiers of the
flesh do we here owe one of the choicest
delicacies of the taste."

Hermitage was formerly much used in Bourdeaux for mixing with the Médoc wines, in giving them more body and tone and qualifying them for the English market. The wines are red, white, and *vins de paille* (straw-coloured) ; the two latter, however, form but a very small proportion. Hermitage requires to be kept in cask from four to six years before bottling, and to this circumstance, as well as to the supply itself being limited, the wine will always maintain a high price. In the department of the Rhône, about seven leagues from Lyons, is grown the famous Côte Rôtie. At the International Exhibition of 1862 M. de la Sizeranne of Gaillac exhibited some Hermitage of the vintage of 1760, combining the vigour and freshness of a young wine with these qualities of age.

The wines of *Burgundy* have long held a high reputation. The district from whence they come extends fifty miles in length, and is formed of the departments of Yonne, Côte d'Or, and Saône et Loire. Both as regards the soil which produces the grape, and the aspect on which so much depends its ripening, the vineyards of the Côte d'Or, as well as others situated between Dijon and Chagny, are highly favoured. It is also the superior skill in the manipulation and the completeness of the fermentation that contribute to this wine the excellence for which it is renowned.

Nuits is fifteen miles south of Dijon, and may be considered as in the midst of the Burgundy district. There are spacious cellars here in which every description of wine grown in the neighbourhood is stored in large quantities.

The principal red wines of Burgundy are *Romanée Conti, Clos-Vougeôt, Chambertin, Corton, Volnay, Pommard, Beaune, Macon, Beaujolais, &c.* The Clos Vougeôt is a vineyard so highly esteemed that when a French regiment marches past, it halts and presents arms. We are informed, however, that " it is much overrated, for although the upper part on the acclivity produces wine such as none other surpasses, still the declivity is not at all equal to it ; and the lowest

part is no better than many other vineyards in the neighbourhood." The extent
of this farm is but eighty acres, and its
average produce about 500 hogsheads ;
whilst that of Romanée Conti is only six
acres and a half, and the produce small in
proportion. Another vineyard of high
repute, Chambertin, is situate in the same
neighbourhood ; its growth is not more
than about 150 hogsheads. With such a
limited produce it cannot be expected that
these very superior wines are frequently to
be met with. But in doing justice to their
merits, we must not for one moment overlook the claims of the other red wines of
Burgundy,—viz. those of Nuits, Volnay,
Pommard, Beaune, Macon, &c. The Volnay is commended for its light and delicate
flavour and tint, whilst Pommard has more
substance and colour ; but they are all
more or less distinguished by great richness and fulness of body, and at the same
time delicacy of flavour and exquisite
aroma, and are certainly entitled to high
respect.

The white wines of Burgundy are less
numerous, and in England they are also
less known.   They are chiefly *Chablis*,
*Pouilly*, *Meursault*, aud the much prized
*Montrachet*.  The wine of Pouilly possesses
a fine *bouquet* and is very agreeable.
Chablis is produced in the Yonne district,
and is better known in England than any
of the others.   It is a very nice clean wine,
very pale in colour, and delicate in flavour.
Oysters and Chablis are a favourite luncheon
with our Gallic neighbours, and as oysters
generally precede a French dinner, they are
on such occasions frequently accompanied
by libations of Chablis.  Indeed we are told,
by those who profess to understand such
matters, that it is one of the wines which
should always be placed first in order at
the dinner table.

M. Jullien informs us that the vineyards
of Burgundy cover an area of 103,000 hectares, the produce, on the average, being
2,550,000 hectolitres* of wine, 70,000 of

---

* The hectolitre contains about 22 English gallons.

which are consumed in the country. The vineyards have increased very much since the Revolution, many landlords having converted into vineyards low and marshy lands; others having introduced manures, or carried new earth upon the old to increase the crop; others again, have substitued young for the old plants.

We have stated in another place that in the earlier times, although by far the largest part of the wine consumed was the produce of our own country, yet for foreign wines we were principally dependent on those of France. In the reign of Charles II. the consumption of French wines was two-fifths that of the whole of England. The favourite vintages were those of Bourdeaux, Burgundy, and Hermitage; for Champagne, although known in this country as early as the time of Henry VIII, did not come into general use till after the Restoration (1660). Patin, writing in 1666, speaks of Louis XIV. making a present to Charles II. of England of two hundred hogsheads of excellent wine, viz.—Champagne, Burgundy,

and Hermitage.    Down to the time of the
Revolution of 1688, great quantities of
French wines were imported.    Mr. Cyrus
Redding says, "The jealousy towards
every thing French after that time, induced the laying on of enormous duties by
legislatures, who were not wise enough to
reflect that those wines must have been
exchanged for British commodities of one
class or another."    Heavy duties had been
levied on French wines from time to time,
until in fifteen years the duty had risen
from 1*s*. 4*d*. to 4*s*. 10*d*. per gallon, being an
increase of 360 per cent. ; and in 1703 the
Methuen treaty was entered into with Portugal, by which we were bound to receive
the wines of that country at one-third less
duty than those of France.    From this
time the importation of French wines was
almost discontinued, and the stock on hand
becoming exhausted, it was found necessary to seek for some substitute for them ;
and the red wines of Portugal, which had
been introduced for the first time into this
country about 1688, established themselves

in supplanting those of France. Since 1831, however, the duty on all foreign wines has been equalized. The following is the rate of duty now chargeable on wines, as proposed by Mr. Gladstone in 1862.

" On and after the 4th April, 1862, and without any allowance for drawback, the following Rates of Duty will be levied on Wine of, or from Foreign countries; also on Wine the growth and produce of any British possessions.

| | Containing less than the following Rates of Proof Spirit, verified by Sikes' Hydrometer, viz. | | If imported in Bottles, and containing less than 42 degrees. |
|---|---|---|---|
| | 26 degrees, | 42 degrees | |
| | *s.* *d.* | *s.* *d.* | *s.* *d.* |
| Red Wine, the gallon | 1 0 | 2 6 | 2 6 |
| White Wine, the gallon | 1 0 | 2 6 | 2 6 |
| Lees of such Wines . . | 1 0 | 2 6 | 2 6 |

And for every degree of strength beyond the highest above specified, an additional duty of 3*d.* per gallon; no more than 10 per cent. of proof Spirit shall be used in the fortifying of any Wine in Bond, nor shall any Wine be fortified in Bond to a greater degree of strength than 40 per cent. of such proof Spirit."

It will be seen from the foregoing statement that French wines, which, from an excessive duty, never had fair play from the year 1697 (when the differential duty was first imposed) to 1831, still labour under a disadvantage in the English market; inasmuch as the commoner sorts being admitted at the shilling duty, and the better descriptions paying 2s. 6d., the former have a manifest advantage to the comparative exclusion of the latter. And taking into account the absurd professions so vauntingly put forward in respect to the "cheap Gladstone wines," and the mendacious advertisements which were heralded forth in consequence, we can scarcely wonder that the question of *quality* is so entirely sacrificed to that of *cheapness.* Nothing but an *equalised* low rate of duty will ever afford the better wines of France an opportunity of being known and appreciated by English tastes. Great credit is due to Mr. Benjamin Oliveira, who, whilst in the House of Commons, annually brought forward a motion to the above effect; but the time and circumstances were both unfavourable to a satisfactory result, inasmuch as the grape disease intervened, and the advent of the Crimean war soon afterwards stood in the way of any reduction of taxation. To Mr. Shaw we are likewise much indebted for his earnest and untiring exertions in favour of a uniform low rate of duty. With much practical knowledge and great experience on the subject, this gentleman many years ago took up the question, at a time when there was a surplus revenue to favour the project. May he live to see his views adopted and successfully worked out !

Regarded both in a commercial and fiscal point of view, it is equally clear that Mr. Gladstone's measure has utterly failed in its object. He has either gone *too far*, or *not far enough*. Too far, from the fact of the revenue having derived no benefit from the reduction of duty, as the non-fulfilment of the pledge to give the public *good* wines has stood in the way of the increased consumption he so ardently anticipated. And not far enough, inasmuch as the 2*s*. 6*d*. differential duty practically shuts out the French wines that are really drinkable; and the 1*s*. duty at the same time admits only those which are thin and sour, indeed in

some instances not equal to bear the sea
passage.

It is alleged by some, that if strongly
brandied wines are allowed to be introduced
at a low rate of duty, they will be converted into spirit, and the Government
defrauded of the duty.   The answer to
this is, that a wine merchant imports only
that which he believes to be marketable;
and if his wine is so fortified that it shall
appear more like brandy, it will be unsaleable.   As to getting it distilled and the
spirit sold profitably as brandy, not even
the most suspicious Customs or Inland
Revenue Officer believes that this can be
done.

We quote the following from the trade
circular of a large firm which has benefited
perhaps more extensively by Mr. Gladstone's enactment than any other house;
we cannot, therefore, refuse to accept their
testimony.   " It would seem, in fact, as if
the fates were against Mr. Gladstone and
his changes.   His endeavour has undoubtedly been to favour the wines of France in

preference to those of Spain and Portugal;
nevertheless, like the prophet of old, he
has been constrained to bless those whom
he was called to curse. His flowing rhetoric
may take captive the minds of his country-
men, and his specious logic may mystify
their understanding, but his thin wines fail
to satisfy their English stomachs. For
although in 1861 he persuaded them to
swallow 2,229,028 gallons of French wine,
in 1863 he could only get them to imbibe
1,939,555 gallons, *being a reduction of*
289,473 gallons, instead of an increase, as
he anticipated; while during the same period
the *consumption of Port and Sherry had
actually increased upwards of four hundred
thousand gallons*, namely from 6,734,503 in
1861, up to 7,150,104 gallons in 1863, or
415,601 gallons of actual increase." The
following is an extract from the circular of
another house dealing also to a great extent
in French wines. " The sale of light wines
has disappointed the very sanguine expectations held by those who have gone into
this class too exclusively. They find it a

work of time to accustom the public palate, even for its summer drink, to the many descriptions now introduced to this country."

Much might be adduced in support of the opinion we have so freely expressed on the subject of differential duties, but our limits will scarcely admit of discussing the matter at greater length; at the same time we feel confident that the question is one which cannot fail to commend itself to the serious consideration of the public. It would be ungracious, however, to express aught but gratitude to Mr. Gladstone for having effected even a partial reduction; nor can we ignore the great attention he has devoted to the subject. We will console ourselves in the hope that the result of some two or three years working of the present system will be sufficient to induce him to apply his vigorous mind to remedy the anomaly of the present rate of duty.

The following account of the famous dispute arising out of the rival claims of Burgundy and Champagne may not be uninteresting. About the middle of the seventeenth century, a regular paper war was commenced in the French schools of science, on the respective merits of Burgundy and Champagne. The controversy arose in consequence of a candidate for medical honours choosing to maintain, in his inaugural thesis, that the wines of Burgundy were preferable to those of Champagne, and that the latter were irritating to the nerves, and productive of dangerous diseases, particularly gout. Of course the Faculty of Medicine at Rheims took up the defence of the Champagne wines, eulogising their purity, brightness, exquisite flavour and *bouquet*, their durability, and superiority to the growths of Burgundy. This produced a rejoinder from the pen of the Professor of the College of Beaune, and the subject was discussed with much warmth, in verse as well as prose; till the national disasters that accompanied the close of Louis XIV's reign directed the public attention to matters of greater importance. However, the controversy was afterwards continued, the world going on in other respects much the same notwithstanding, until 1778, about 130 years from the commencement of the dispute, when, in a thesis defended before the Faculty of Medicine at Paris, a verdict was ultimately pronounced in favour of the vintage of Champagne.

The fine old town of Rheims, in the department of the Marne, may be considered as the centre of the *Champagne* growing district.

The produce of the Marne may be divided into two classes,—the River Wines and the Mountain Wines. The best River Wines are obtained from the vineyards situated in the valleys, and on the sides of the hills that border the Marne at Aï, Hautvilliers, Epernay, Dizy, Avernay, &c. Of the Rheims Mountain Wines, those of Vezey, Verzenay, Mailly, and Bouzy are most esteemed.

The wine cannot, as in the case of other wines, be described under particular growths, the pressings being generally mixed one sort with another, so that the vinous properties deficient in one class are supplied by another; whilst the reputation of particular brands is acquired chiefly by superior management, as well as greater facilities of selecting such fruit or pressings as are adapted to the requirements; for it must be borne in mind that many of the proprietors have to purchase largely beyond the actual produce of their own vineyards.

The operation of pressing the grapes is performed as rapidly as possible. The three first pressures produce the choicest, which is put aside. A few houses will only admit into their *cuvées* or bins these three pressures (which probably do not yield above three-fifths of the juice of the grape), rejecting the remaining pressings, or reserving them for use in the preparation of the inferior descriptions of wine.

The *bouquet* of wine is altogether a new product, and is in no way dependent on the perfume of the grape from which the wine is made. The ordinary way of giving the requisite *bouquet* in the manufacture of Champagne is to prepare a syrup composed of orris root (Iris Florentina), brandy, and sugar candy; and a minute portion of this is poured into each cask generally after the first fermentation has subsided. The best account of the *bouquet* of wine is given by Liebig, who says,—" It is well known that wine and fermented liquors generally contain, in addition to alcohol, other substances which could not be detected before their fermentation, and which must have been formed during that process. The smell and taste which distinguish wine from all other fermented liquids are known to depend on an æther of a volatile and highly combustible acid, which is of an oily nature, and to which the name of *œnanthic æther* has been given. This product possesses, in like manner as sugar, equal proportions of carbon and hydrogen, but differing from sugar in the amount of its oxygen."

The bottling takes place in March, and the fermentation commences about May. The latter continues all the summer, but is particularly strong in June during the flowering of the vine, and in August when the fruit begins to ripen. At these times the greatest loss in the bursting of bottles takes place, averaging from 10 to 15 and even from 30 to 40 per cent. It is not safe to pass through a cellar without being guarded with a mask of iron wire, and it occasionally happens that the workmen who disregard this precaution are severely injured. Such is the uncertainty attending the process of fermentation, that of two piles of the same wine, in the same cellar, scarcely a bottle will be left of one, whilst the other remains comparatively uninjured. In the necks of the bottles, which are inverted in racks, there is always a sediment, which it is necessary to remove. This is done by a peculiar manipulation termed *dégorgement.* Each bottle is taken by the bottom, kept carefully in its reversed position, and the wire and twine being broken, whilst the bottle rests between the workman's knees, the cork is dexterously withdrawn, so as to allow the gas to explode, carrying the deposit with it. It is possible that this process may have to be repeated

a second and even a third time; so that the
losses sustained by these operations, and by
the bursting of the bottles, are certainly
equal to 20 per cent.

The first rank is usually assigned to the
wines of Sillery, under which name is com-
prehended the produce of the vineyards of
Verzenay, Mailly, Raument, &c. Besides
these there are others celebrated for their
exquisite delicacy of flavour and durability
of quality.

Among the wines prepared to effervesce—
or, to use the technical phrase, for *la mousse*
—there are some which only partake of a
slight fermentation. These are the *cremant*
wines, which drive out the cork with less
force and cream in the glass. Their *mousse*
is frothy, and they are said to have the
advantage over the *Vins grand mousseux*,
in preserving more vinous properties and
being less sharp. Their price is likewise
higher, for they are sought for by con-
noisseurs, and cannot be obtained in great
quantity. It were useless to particularize
every variety of wine known as Cham-

pagne. Some of the lower qualities are so bad that they will not bear exportation.

M. Jullien, in his ' Topographie de Vignobles,' speaking of the cost of production, says, " The high price of the *Vins Mousseux* comes not only from the quality of the wines chosen to make them, and the infinite pains required before they are finished, but also from the considerable losses to which the proprietors and dealers are exposed in this kind of speculation, and the strange phenomena which determine or destroy the *qualité mousseuse.* As to losses, the owners count in general upon fifteen or twenty bottles broken in a hundred ; sometimes even thirty or forty. To this must be added the diminution which takes place as the wine is separated from its deposits by decanting,—an operation which is performed at least twice."

The high appreciation in which Champagne is held may be traced as far back as the thirteenth century, and indeed earlier. Even princes and sovereigns of other countries have not only admired and partaken of this exquisite delicacy, but have become *producers* as well as *consumers;* inasmuch as Francis I. of France, Pope Leo X., Charles V. of Spain, and Henry VIII. of England possessed vineyards at Aï as their exclusive property, retaining resident super-intendents to secure the genuine produce, each for his own table.

Champagne, when well made, and placed in cellars of a proper temperature, will retain its quality for ten or twenty years. Indeed it has been known to keep for even fifty years, but we must be understood to refer exclusively to wines of a high standard of quality.

The vaults at Rheims, Avize, and Eper-nay, are of great extent, and the value of the wines stored in the *cuvées* therein is immense; and yet we are told "it was only in the year 1780, that when a merchant at Epernay made 6000 bottles (500 dozens), he was considered a daring speculator." The produce of last year is given at 10,705,207 bottles.

The intoxicating effects of Champagne

are rapid, but exceedingly transient. This
arises partly from the carbonic acid which
is evolved from it, and partly from its
alcohol, which being suspended in the gas,
extends itself rapidly over the surface of
the stomach. As a remedial agent the
virtues of Champagne must not be overlooked, since it is largely employed by
medical men as a restorative in cases of
great prostration of strength.

Diversity of opinion exists as to the de-
sirability of icing Champagne. When so
much depends on the state of the weather,
as well as on the temperature of the cellar
from whence the wine is brought, it will be
found impossible to fix a particular rule;
and as we purpose entering more fully into
this subject in a future chapter having
reference to the cellar and to the general
management of wines, we will merely suggest here that in the hottest weather nor
under any circumstances should the bottle
be kept on the ice for more than a quarter
of an hour; feeling assured that the wine
is frequently much deteriorated by an in-

tense degree of cold. The practice of putting ice *into* the Champagne is, having regard to the quality of the wine, too absurd a one to treat of seriously. Care should be taken with all effervescent wines, that in storing them away, the bottles should be laid down, for if they are allowed to remain upright the corks become dry, and admit of the escape of the gas as well as of the admission of air, and the wine rapidly spoils in consequence.

Before we dismiss the subject of Champagne, we will briefly refer to two useful inventions, which we recommend to the notice of the connoisseur. One is a light metal frame in which the bottle is placed, and having a handle obviates the necessity of grasping the bottle with the warm hand in pouring out the wine. The other is an elastic stopper, consisting of a screw stem,

with a nut at one end and a bulb at the other, passing through an india-rubber collar. By turning the nut the screw is drawn up, and the elastic collar so pressed by the bulb against the contraction in the gullet of the bottle as effectually to resist any escape, whilst by means of a tap and air pipe any portion of the wine can be drawn off without withdrawing the cork; thus after partaking of a glass or two of " sparkling," the ullage may be preserved in its pristine state; to the invalid who may be ordered to take a glass or two of Champagne daily, this little apparatus is extremely valuable. These useful articles are to be had of the manufacturers, Messrs. Farrow and Jackson, of Great Tower Street.

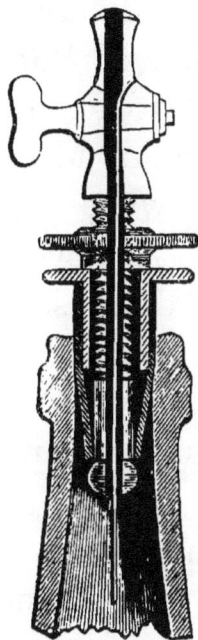

*Masdeu* is a wine the produce of vineyards between Perpignan and Collioure, the property of Messrs. Durand, the well-known bankers of Paris and Perpignan, and was introduced into this country about forty years since with rather indifferent success; but the upward tendency of Port some few years afterwards led to an increased consumption in the article of Masdeu, which was largely mixed with, and even substituted for, Port wine. Although of late years the consumption has decreased, yet at the present time no pains or expense are spared to perfect the quality; we are of opinion, however, that it has served its purpose in days gone by.

It is in this neighbourhood that the *muscadine* wines are grown; they are distinguished as being very luscious, spirituous, and richly fragrant. Foremost in this class are the wines of *Rivesaltes, Salces, Frontignan,* and *Lunel;* the latter is very sweet, possesses great strength, and is chiefly used as a *liqueur.*

The grape blight, which was first observed in a gentleman's vinery at Margate in 1845, made its appearance in France in 1850, when it infected some of the vineyards in the neighbourhood of Paris. In

1851 it became general throughout all France, and obtained its maximum of intensity in 1854. It is a sort of fungus called *oidium* which constitutes the disease. Its ravages were severely felt during its continuance, and to such a height had its virulence extended, that in 1854 the vintage had diminished to about one-fourth of the average quantity. In 1855 the practice of sulphuring the vines became general, and from that year may be dated the arrest of the disease and its ultimate disappearance. Sulphur appears to act directly on the fungus, withering and decomposing it in a few hours; charcoal has also been found to possess the same efficacy, arising doubtless from its absorbent and antiseptic properties. The grape blight cannot, therefore, be considered a permanent obstacle to the production of wine; it may occasionally appear and do some damage, but it is now under control, and will henceforth only rank amongst the many causes which may, under certain circumstances, exercise, more or less, an unfavourable influence upon the vintage of a particular year.

The Halle aux Vins, or wine-market, is
one of the most complete and best arranged
of any of the places in Paris for the accom-
modation of merchants and traders.  It is
situated at Bercey, within the walls of the
capital, at its eastern extremity, beyond the
Jardin des Plantes.  The inconvenience of
the old Halle, established in 1656, had
long been felt; but the first stone of the
present market was not laid until the 15th
of August, 1813, when the Empire was in
its wane.  At first the works were actively
carried on, but political disasters occasioned
them to be suspended, and they were not
completed until several years after the Restoration.  It fronts the river.  The piles
of magazines are seven in number, four in
front and three behind.  The two centre
piles in the front are divided into seven
compartments, and are used as a market.
One of the buildings in the back division is
of large dimensions for containing brandy.
The buildings are neat and commodious,
and a part of them are surrounded by
a terrace.  The space between the different
masses forms a sort of street, of which

there are several, named after various kinds
of wine—as the Rue de Champagne, Rue
de Bourgogne, Rue de Bourdeaux, Rue de
Languedoc, Rue de la Côte d'Or. This
latter street is the finest, and extends the
whole length of the *halle.* There are
counting-houses for the merchants, and
small *bureaux* for the officers who super-
intend the entrance and delivery of the
wines. The rent charged is about 10*d.* per
hogshead per annum, and the *octroi* and
other town dues amount to about 10*d.* per
gallon ; the number of entries sometimes
amounts to 1500 a day.

It was formerly the custom with proprietors of small vineyards to cause their
wines to be announced by the public crier,
and those who wished to purchase carried
a pot with them to contain the article ;
hence the expression, *vendre à pot.* In
case a difficulty was experienced in the
sale of their wines, the growers would
sometimes elect to dispose of them by
retail ; in this case they suspended over
the door, or from a window, a broom, a

crown of ivy, or something similar. Ivy was rather used than any other plant, it being considered illustrative of Bacchus. This custom eventually led to the well known practice of distinguishing the *cabarets* or wine shops in different parts of France* by having a bough or part of a tree suspended, sometimes decorated with flowers, ribbons, fruit, &c., so that the trade or calling might be at once seen. And this custom of displaying a bush or branch outside of the houses of retailers of wine has given origin to the old proverb of " Good wine needs no bush."

---

* The subjoined passages prove the custom to have existed in this country also :—

   " Green ivy-bushes at the vintners' doores."

     ' *Summers' Last Will and Testament.*' 1600.

   " 'Tis like the ivy-bush unto a tavern."

     ' *Rival Friends.*' 1632.

# CHAPTER XII.

## WINES OF SPAIN.

" Give me sacke, old sacke, boys,
 To make the muses merry;
 The life of mirth, and the joy of the earth,
 Is a cup of good old sherry."
 PASQUIL's ' *Palinodia.*' (1619).

" Adieu, fair Cadiz! yea, a long adieu!
 Who may forget how well thy walls have stood?
 When all wert changing, thou alone wert true,
 First to be free and last to be subdued."
 BYRON. ' *Childe Harold,*' *canto* i, *st.* 85.

PAIN occupies the greater part of that peninsula which is divided from France by the mountain-range of the Pyrenees, and its area is stated to be nearly 190,000 square miles. The coast-line is 1370 miles, of which 602 are washed by the Atlantic and 768 by the Mediterranean.

The climate of Spain is one of the most genial for the culture of the grape, and the wines of that country deservedly rank high, not only in England, but throughout the world.

The word *Sherry* is derived from the name of the town Xeres, or as it is called Xeres de la Frontera, to distinguish it from other towns of the same name in the interior, one of the wealthiest in Spain, situate in the ancient province of Andalusia, twenty miles from Cadiz, on the direct line of railway from that place passing through Cordova on to Madrid, which was opened throughout in August of the present year.

Sherry is undoubtedly the first of Spanish wines, and is grown almost exclusively in the districts between Xeres and San Lucar, every available piece of ground being appropriated to that purpose; although wines are brought from Malaga and other places, and shipped at Cadiz, which have no affinity to Sherry wine except in name. The highest classed Sherries are celebrated for their delicate character and great dryness. Among these may be instanced the *Amontillado*, which has long been held in high repute, and the *Vino de Pasto*, or as the term implies, *wine of breakfast*, or repast. Its growth is not confined to any particular locality, it being selected from any that may appear to recommend themselves. There are other first growth wines distinguished for their high quality. The *Soleras*, so called, are the fine old mother wines, which by age, care, and attention have acquired both fulness of body and concentrated aroma; they are much in use for toning and improving other and newer wines. The wine is generally brought down the country in leathern vessels, or, as the Spaniards call them, *boots*, whence we derive our term butts,* the casks in which the wine is contained.

Immense stocks are kept at Xeres and Cadiz; that of one merchant alone is said to be 15,000 butts, and his vineyard at Macharnudo is considered the finest in the district. This gentleman, referring to Sherry, writes, "The consumers seldom

---

* A butt of Sherry is 108 gallons.

get bad wines but when they choose for themselves. Sherries of a deep colour contain a portion of concentrated brown wine, which supplies the place of brandy; whereas, common-place wines must be highly brandied, and are much more fiery than wines of colour; but whether pale or brown, the lowest wine sent from Spain is always the juice of the grape. It may be the produce of bad seasons or bad growth, but in Spain adulteration is wholly unknown. The colouring of Sherry is Sherry, and all the brandy the wine contains is made from Sherry. The uniformly sustained quality of Sherry wine, where price is given, arises from the fact that in the best grounds in Spain the vintage never entirely fails. The produce of the more remarkable vintages, as far as it comes to the Xeres market, is entirely absorbed by the principal shippers, whose brands are familiar to you."

The wines of *Montilla*, in the neighbouring province of Cordova, are also justly celebrated; they rank among the finest produce of Spain for their delicacy and purity. *Manzanilla*, grown on the plains towards the Guadalquiver, is a wine of much character, and is highly prized by the inhabitants of the country, for although the produce is considerable, only a comparatively small portion appears to be exported. *Mountain* is a sweet luscious wine, possessing great body and strength, and is the produce of Malaga in the province of Granada; although formerly very extensively used, it is in little demand at the present day. We read of some bottles of this wine, buried at the time of the fire of London and disinterred in 1811, the quality of which was said to be excellent. We have reason to believe that the Spanish wines of two or three centuries back were principally the produce of the Malaga districts, until the latter were superseded by the superior quality of the wines of Cadiz and Xeres. In Andalusia is grown the wine termed *Rota Tinto*, or more familiarly known in England as *Tent;* it is a rich red wine, and is occasionally used by invalids as a stomachic; it is also the

sacramental wine employed in the adminis-
tration of the communion. In this district
also is produced *Paxarêtê*, a sweet wine
but little known. At Manzares, situate
in the province of La Mancha, the much
esteemed *Val de Penas* is made. It is a
red wine, and grown on rocky or stony
ground, whence its name of *valley of stones.*
It is much in request by the Spaniards,
who prize this wine and the Manzanilla
above referred to much more highly than
the wines of Xeres themselves. The
province of Valencia supplies in considerable quantity a strong and full flavoured
red wine called *Benicarlo.* This wine, as
well as the wines of the adjacent district of
Alicant, constitute the article known by
the trade as "*Spanish Reds,*" so largely
called upon at the present day to do duty
for Port wine. They are also shipped to
France and extensively used in the preparation of Claret for "the English market."

Much uncertainty exists at the present
day as to the precise nature of the wine so
familiarly spoken of by Shakspeare and

others under the name of *Sack*. The popular impression is that it was a dry wine,
and that it took its name from the French
word *sec*, or dry. This derivation, nevertheless, is somewhat questionable, inasmuch
as dry Sherry was scarcely, if at all, known
in those days ; the wines in common use
prior to that time being exclusively sweet
wines. The rendering given by Minchin,
and also by Colgrave, is *sec*, dry wine ; and
the former describes it as " a wine that
comes out of Spain." Skinner and Man-
delslo, on the contrary, assert that it takes
its name from Xique, a town of Morocco.
An Act passed in the reign of Henry VIII.
speaks of " sakkes and other sweete wines,"
and in Beaumont and Fletcher's Comedy
of ' Rule a Wife and have a Wife,' we read,
" Give me a cup of sack, an ocean of sweet
sack." Falstaff, in the First Part of
Henry IV, Act ii. scene 4, says, "You
rogue, here's *lime* in this Sack, too ; there
is nothing but roguery to be found in
villainous man : yet a coward is worse than
a cup of sack with lime in it." Now as

H

lime is used in the manufacture of Sherry
to conduce to its well known dry quality
by neutralizing a portion of the *malic* or
*tartaric* acid, it has been conjectured that
the Sack referred to could be no other
than Sherry wine. Dr. Henderson states
that Sack was a wine exported from Spain,
probably the dry wine of Xeres then imported for the first time into England ; and
suggests the hypothesis that it derived its
name from the Spanish term, *vino sacco*,
signifying export wine. However, whether
Sack were dry or sweet, or whether there
were two varieties of the wine, it is evident that it was not the produce of one
locality alone, for in an old play we find,
" Some wine, boy ! Sack ! Canary Sack !"
and Ben Jonson speaks of his receiving a
present of Palm Sack, or Sack from the
island of Palma. Markham also says,
" Your best Sacks are of Xeres in Spain ;
your smaller of Gallicia and Portugal ; your
strong Sacks are of the Canaries and Mal-
ligo ; and your Muscadans and Malmseys
are of many parts of Italy, Greece, and

some special islands." Now as we know that the term Malmsey was applied to the sweet wines of Tyre, Candia, Italy, Greece, and the various islands of the Archipelago indiscriminately, we are led to believe, that in like manner, although the term Sack, in its strictest and literal sense, might have been meant to imply dry wine, from the fact of "Sweet Sacks" being mentioned also, yet that, from common use, it became the generic name under which the white wines of that day were ordinarily recognized. In 1667, the price, as fixed at Oxford, was "Sack and Malagaes one shilling the quart, and no more." Those who are curious in such matters will find in an old volume of Songs and Ballads, written in the time of Charles II., entitled 'Wit's Recreations' (1640), a quaint old ditty, called *A Song in Praise of Sack*, also one in reply, *The Answer of Ale to the Challenge of Sack*, which in its turn is followed by another, *The Tryumph of Tobacco over Sack and Ale.* In a volume of poems published in 1719, called 'Wit and Mirth, or Pills to Purge

Melancholy,' written and collected by Tho-
mas D'Urfey, we find several Ballads of a
like nature, viz. :—*The Jovial Drinker,
Old English Ale, A Song in Praise of
Punch, The Reformed Drinker,* and one,
*On the Virtues of Sack,* commencing

" Fetch me Ben Jonson's skull, and fill't with Sack," &c.

This collection of poems is esteemed by
bibliographers for its scarceness, and fetches
a high price ; its finest points, however, are
sadly marred by the coarseness of phrase-
ology peculiar to the period.   The writer
died in 1723, and was buried at St. James',
Westminster, where a small slab let into
the wall simply records the name,

| TOM D'URFEY. |

Rain is comparatively scarce on the table-
land of Spain ; it is stated that the annual
quantity on an average does not amount
to more than ten inches.   Near Alicant
reservoirs for the irrigation of the vine

grounds have been constructed on a large scale. About twelve miles from the town a tank is formed by damming up a valley with an embankment 240 feet high, and 40 thick. This supplies water for an entire year. Others, though of smaller dimensions, are established in suitable localities; but these are very inadequate towards furnishing the requisite supply of water in very dry seasons. This is much felt in some districts; and so oppressive was the drought and equally abundant the vintage of 1858, that at Huesca, in Arragon, an extensive proprietor considered it would have been easier and cheaper to irrigate his vineyards with wine than with water. At Aranda del Duero, in Old Castile, wine would also seem to be occasionally cheaper than water; for an English gentleman, travelling through that province, witnessed some bricklayers at work mixing their mortar with wine instead of water; and this, we are informed, was no unusual occurrence, as there were several instances of houses in that town having been built with mortar prepared in this way.* The town-hall of Toro, in the province of Leon, is likewise said to have been erected with mortar slaked with wine, and for a similar reason. This reminds us of a passage in the Epigrams of Martial, referring to the scarcity of water in those days, wherein the poet says he would rather have a cistern at Ravenna than a vineyard, since the water would fetch a higher price than the wine; and adds that a shrewd innkeeper at Ravenna lately imposed on him, for on asking for wine and water he was supplied with the full quantity of wine only.

> " Sit cisterna mihi, quam vinea, malo Ravennæ:
>   Cum possim multo vendere pluris aquam."
>     Martial. *Epigrammata, Book* iii, *Epig.* 56.
> " Calidus imposuit nuper mihi caupo Ravennæ
>   Cum peterem mixtum, vendidit ille merum."
>     *The same, Epig.* 57.

These two or three anecdotes will tend to

---

* Both these anecdotes rest on the authority of Mr. Lumley, Her Majesty's Secretary of the Spanish Legation, as given in his official report to the Foreign Office, on the Commerce of Spain. — *Vide Parliamentary Report,*— ' *Secretaries of Embassies,*' 1860.

impress us with the value of the article of water, which, whilst blest with a plentiful supply, we are apt to undervalue, but which in times of drought and scarcity cannot be over estimated; and if we may be considered as having drawn on the credulity of our readers in quoting facts which bear the stamp of authority, let those who incline to that opinion read the following little article on the hidden properties of water, copied from the ' Athenæum.' It is headed ' Fire from Water.' " Some persons are reported to have discovered that caloric is abundant in cold water, and that when coal fails we shall have to burn up our rivers! A bucket of water will be called for instead of a scuttle of coal, and it will be a question with tee-totallers whether water will be a lawful beverage, since philosophy will have demonstrated it to be nothing less than ' liquid fire.' "

In Spain the effects of the *oidium*, the nature of which is more fully described in the preceding chapter, were severely felt throughout the kingdom, and in some dis-

tricts the failure was so complete, that many
of the growers were, for several seasons,
unable to pay any rent.  It first appeared
in 1852.  Vines near the coast and on the
banks of rivers suffered most; but those
on higher soils, and even in the mountains
did not wholly escape.

For a considerable time Spain derived
much of its prosperity from its trade with
the Spanish American colonies.  Previous
to 1720, the monopoly of this trade was
enjoyed by Seville, but in that year it was
removed to Cadiz, which soon became one
of the most opulent cities of Europe,
foreigners of all nations having factories ·
and business houses there.  This commercial activity, however, was greatly checked
by the war of 1793, and has since been
wholly destroyed through the defection of
the Spanish possessions in America.  In
the days of its prosperity, it is said that
Cadiz hardly contained a person incapable
of supporting himself, which state of things
was so far altered, that a writer travelling
through Spain in 1835, informs us that

"scarce may one go forth into the streets by day or night without being pursued by crowds of beggars, and not unfrequently by women decently dressed, who still preserve a semblance of their former elegance, though begging their daily bread." Since that time, however, and more especially during the last seven or eight years, Spain has made rapid strides in the march of prosperity, and should she continue to progress in the same ratio, we may expect to see her, at no very distant period, restored to the proud commercial rank she so long occupied among the nations of Europe.

Notwithstanding the great encouragement given to French, German, and other light wines, Sherry has not only maintained its position, but the shipments of 1863 exceed those of the previous year by 13,603 butts. The following is the number of gallons entered for Home Consumption during the last seven years; shewing, notwithstanding the admission of the lower class wines at the shilling duty on January 1st, 1861, an average increase on Sherry of 1,197,227 gallons for the last three years.

| | |
|---|---|
| 1857 . . . . | 2,776,964 |
| 1858 . . . . | 2,657,131 |
| 1859 . . . . | 2,876,554 |
| 1860 . . . . | 2,975,906 |
| 1861 . . . . | 4,031,796 |
| 1862 . . . . | 3,956,213 |
| 1863 . . . . | 4,531,424 |

The entire produce of wine in Spain is estimated at an average of about 135,000,000 gallons.

# CHAPTER XIII.

On the Wines of Portugal.

" Few things surpass old wine ; and they may preach
Who please,—the more because they preach in vain,—
Let us have wine."
            Byron. *'Don Juan,' canto* ii. *st.* 178.

" Of all drinks wine is most profitable, of medicines
most pleasant, and of dainty viands most harmless; provided always that it b̈e well tempered with opportunity
of the time."—Plutarch's *' Moralia.'*

ortugal is the most westerly kingdom of Europe. It forms part of
the Spanish peninsula, and is not divided
from Spain by any well-defined natural
boundaries. All the great rivers of Portugal, the Minho, the Douro, the Tagus,
aud the Guadiana, have their sources in
Spain, and belong to Portugal only in the
lower part of their basins. Its area is
reckoned at about 37,900 square miles ; it
has a coast line of about 500 miles bounded

by the Atlantic, of which about 400 miles face the west.

Portugal, as well from its geographical position and geological conformation as from other propitious circumstances, appears to have been destined for the development and perfection of the vine. This natural superiority, however, has been sadly marred by the indolence and ignorance of the cultivators, for the produce might have been vastly increased and still more improved, and ordinary wines have acquired a better character, if the farmers, instead of sluggishly allowing themselves to become the slaves of custom, had studied the mode of culture best suited to the plant, and availed themselves of the progressive improvements which modern science dictates in the manufacture of the wine itself.

Although Lisbon white wines had been known in England at an earlier period, it is evident that the red wines of Portugal were not introduced till about 1688; nor were the Portuguese at that time celebrated for either the quality or extent of their growth of wine. But external events

were effecting for Portugal what she was
incapable of doing for herself. A jealous
rivalry and national animosity had long
existed in the councils of England and
France, which gradually increasing in as-
perity, by fiscal regulations and prohibitions
operated most injuriously on the commerce
of the respective countries, and finally led
to open hostilities. The red wines of
France had up to that time been extensively used in England, but the hatred
towards France, and indeed to every thing
French, led to heavy duties being laid on
the wines of that country, until in fifteen
years the duty of French wines had risen
from 1*s.* 4*d.* to 4*s.* 10*d.* per gallon. And
the Methuen treaty entered into with Portugal in 1703, by which we agreed to
receive the wines of that country at one-
third less than those of France, effectually
excluded the latter from the English market. The injustice as well as the impolicy
of such a measure will not now be denied ;
its tendency was to check the admission of
better and cheaper wines, and to create a
giant monopoly. Since 1831, however, the

rate of duty on *all foreign wines has been equalized,—the only inequality at present being in the amount of duty payable on wines of *certain strengths.* Our opinions on this subject have been stated so fully in a preceding chapter that we scarcely need repeat them here, feeling confident that the question must, sooner or later, engage the attention of the thinking portion of the community.

We have shewn that legislation alone forced the wines of Portugal, and especially the red wines of Oporto, into the English market. The taste of the country, however, was not speedily reconciled to the change from the light and exhilarating wines of France to those of a heavier character;

---

* The reader will find it stated elsewhere that in 1831 the duty on all foreign wines was fixed at 5s. 6d. and on Cape wines 2s. 9d.; in 1840 the former were made 5s. 9d. and the latter 2s. 11d.; and in 1860 the latter were assimilated with the former at 5s. 9d. On January 1, 1861, the alcoholic test scale came into operation, and the duty was levied at 1s., 1s. 9d., 2s. 5d. and 2s. 11d. according to the strength. This was altered in 1862 to 1s. and 2s. 6d., being the duty now charged. *(See page 69.)*

and the novel imports were for some time received with undisguised scorn and reluctance. This is illustrated in the 'Farewell to Wine,' 1693, by the following tavern dialogue :—

> " Some Claret, boy !"
> " Indeed, sir, we have none.
> Claret, sir ? Lord ! there's not a drop in town.
> But we have the best red Port."
> " What's that you call
> *Red Port ?*"
> " A wine, sir, comes from Portugal.
> I'll fetch a pint, sir." * * *
> " Ah ! how it smells ! Methinks a real pain
> Is by its odour thrown upon my brain.
> I've tasted it : 'tis spiritless and flat,
> And has as many different tastes,
> As can be found in compound pastes."

The poet Prior also indulges in a fling at the recently imported innovation, as may be seen in the following couplets from his ' Alma.'

> " And in a cottage or a court,
> Drink fine Champagne or *muddled Port*."

> " Else (dismal thought) our warlike men
> Might drink *thick Port* for fine Champagne."

Again, in his ' Cameleon,' we read,—

> " Or if it be his fate to meet
> With folks who have more wealth than wit,
> He love's *cheap Port* and double bub,
> And settles in the Humdrum club."

Whilst Shenstone, in his well-known verses
"written at a tavern in Henley," aims a
shaft in the same direction :—

> " And every health which I begin
> Converts *dull Port* to bright Champagne,—
> Such freedom crown'd it at an inn."

Notwithstanding this coyness in the first
instance, the national prejudice against *Port*
wine gradually subsided, and in the course
of a few years it was enabled to establish
itself into general favour.   By 1720, this
treaty arrangement had conferred an advantage on our new ally over the produce
of the other states equivalent to £24. per
pipe ; and thus compelled, in a manner, to
resort to the wines of Portugal, there is
little need to seek for other reasons why
Port became ultimately the British standard of vinous merit ; and this fact clearly
demonstrates how much may be done by
treaties and taxation in influencing the
tastes and habits of a nation.

Port wine has for nearly two centuries
maintained its pride of place, and may be
said to have thoroughly identified itself
with English palates.   Who is there that

does not remember in the paternal home, his honoured sire's veneration for the rare old " bee's-wing," and for that " particular bin" of "old peculiar?" Brande says, "Good Port wine, duly kept, is, when taken in moderation, one of the most wholesome of vinous liquors ; it strengthens the muscular system, assists the digestive powers, accelerates the circulation, exhilarates the spirits, and sharpens the mental energies. In excess, it is, perhaps, the most mischievous of wines, and most likely to produce those permanent derangements of the digestive organs which follow the habitual use of distilled spirits." That it has not always a tendency to shorten existence, is shewn by the following story of a hearty old squire of the last century, who lived to a good old age. Sir John Sinclair relates, in his ' Code of Health,' that a Mr. Vanhorn, in the space of twenty-three years, drank 36,688 bottles, or 59 pipes of Port wine, furnishing an average daily quota of nearly four bottles and a half. We also read of a citizen of ancient Rome, who ac-

quired the surname of Bicongii, derived
from the word *congius,* a gallon, from the
fact of his being able to imbibe two gallons
of wine at a sitting; and Darius, we are
informed by Athenæus, desired no better
epitaph than that he was able to drink a
great quantity of wine without being inebri-
ated. Dr. Johnson was amongst the ad-
mirers of Port wine, the potency of which
appears to him to have been its chief merit.
There is a table anecdote current, which
makes him say—" Claret for boys, Port for
men, and Brandy for heroes!" The following curious circumstance, which we
think worth recording, is extracted from an
article in the ' Quarterly Review,' entitled
' Wills and Will-making, Ancient and Modern.' A codicil to David Hume's* will
runs thus :—" I leave to my old friend,
Mr. John Home,† of Kilduff, ten dozen of
my old Claret, at his choice, and one single
bottle of that other liquor called Port. I also

---

* The celebrated historian.
† The author of the tragedy of ' Douglas.'

leave to him six dozen of Port, provided
that he attests under his hand, signed
' John Hume,' " that he has himself alone
finished that bottle at two sittings. By
this concession he will at once terminate
the only two differences that ever arose between us concerning temporal affairs." The
" two differences " had reference to the proper mode of spelling their name—whether
" Hume" or " Home,"—and to the merits
of Port wine, which John Home detested.

There is little doubt but that Port, on its
first introduction here, was a much lighter
wine than it afterwards became ; but an
increased consumption and a demand for
wines of fuller body led to the practice of
extensively mixing brandy with the shipments intended for English use. In 1844,
the wine trade was startled from its pro-
priety by the appearance of a pamphlet
entitled 'A Word or Two upon Port Wine,'
from which we extract as follows :—" To
produce black, strong, and sweet wine, the
following are the expedients resorted to :—
The grapes, sound and unsound, are thrown

with the stalks into the vat indiscriminately;
they are then completely smashed, and left
to ferment. When the wine is about half
fermented, it is transferred from the vat to
tonels, and brandy (several degrees above
proof) is thrown in, in the proportion of
twelve to twenty-five gallons to the pipe of
*must*, by which the fermentation is generally
checked. About two months afterwards,
this mixture is coloured thus :—A quantity
of dried elder-berries* is put into coarse
bags, these are placed in vats, and a part
of the wine to be coloured being thrown
over them, the whole of the colouring
matter is expressed, and the husks thrown
away. The dye thus formed is applied
according to the fancy of the owner,
from twenty-eight to fifty-six pounds of the
dried elder-berries being used to the pipe
of wine! Another addition of brandy, of

---

* In justice to the wine-growers, it must be stated, that in
order to remove any ground for such a charge, they obtained,
through the Wine Company of Portugal, a legislative
enactment, which provided that all the trees producing
this berry should be rooted out and their growth prohibited
throughout the wine district.

from four to six gallons per pipe, is now made to the mixture, which is then allowed to rest for about two months. At the end of this time, it is, if sold (which it is tolerably sure to be after such judicious treatment), transferred to Oporto, when it is racked two or three times, and receives, probably, two gallons more of brandy per pipe ; and it is then considered fit to be shipped to England, it being about nine months old. At the time of shipment one gallon more of brandy is usually added to each pipe. The wine thus having received at least twenty gallons of brandy per pipe, is considered by the merchant sufficiently strong, an opinion which the writer at least is not prepared to dispute." The author of the work we quote from met with the bitterest invectives, and meetings were held in Oporto at which resolutions were passed declaring his assertions to be false and unfounded. The writer of the pamphlet subsequently declared himself as Mr. Joseph J. Forrester (Baron de Forrester in Portugal), a man of eminence, and the author

of several important works upon Portugal
and its capabilities, a wine-grower on his
own estate, an exporting merchant, and at
that time a partner in the well-known firm
of Offley, Webber, and Forrester. We
regret to add that Mr. Forrester was accidentally drowned in the Douro on the 12th
May, 1861.

Although there may be much truth in
the statement, yet we must bear in mind
the old saying of "two of a trade;" and
we cannot refrain from regarding the charge
as somewhat exaggerated; and even, if it
be true, the fault must principally rest on
those who created a demand for a manufactured article in preference to a genuine
wine. Thus we see, by a letter addressed
to their agents in the Alto Douro so far
back as 1754, the English factors complain
that "the grower, at the time of the vintage,
is in the habit of checking the fermentation
of the wines too soon, by putting brandy
into them whilst fermenting." The agents,
in reply, assert that "the English merchants
knew that the wine of the Factory had

become excellent; but they wished it to exceed the limits which nature had assigned to it, and that when drunk, it should feel like liquid fire in the stomach; that it should burn like inflamed gunpowder; that it should have the tint of ink; that it should be like the sugar of Brazil in sweetness, and like the spices of India in aromatic flavour. They began by recommending, by way of secret, that it was proper to dash it with brandy in the fermentation to give it strength, and with elder-berries, or the rind of the grape, to give it colour; and as the persons who used the prescription found the wine increase in price, and the English merchants still complaining of a want of strength, colour, and maturity in the article supplied, the recipe was propagated till the wine became a mere confusion of mixtures." We quote the following from a recent work, with a view of showing that the pure wines had ceased to be appreciated and to what extent the demand had arisen for the "black strap" of Port wine drinkers. "Many may still remember ———, than whom no

man was a better judge of port; he kept
resolutely to fine old wine, and would have
nothing to do with the dark strong wines
then in vogue; so he could get no orders,
and his stock, when sold by auction, fetched
only about £20 per pipe. Somewhat later,
the well-known house of ———, noted for
fine old ports lighter than the usual shipments, sold their stock by auction, and what
was the result? an average price of £17.
or £18. per pipe. Rarely have finer wines
been imported than Baron Forrester himself
shipped in conjunction with his old firm;
but dealers wanted colour, strength, and
dryness, *alias* harshness, and even his best
were sold at very low prices." In the
following sentence we find the growers in
1858, having a regard to the quality of the
wine as well as to their own reputation,
petitioning the Portuguese government to
interfere and prevent the shipment of bad
wine :—" The Douro farmers are of opinion
that the promptest and most efficacious
measures for establishing the commercial
credit of Oporto would be to examine every

pipe of port wine actually existing in the merchants' stocks, approved and legalized for exportation; to purify these deposits, and to reduce the rejected wines to brandy, or to sell them in this country (Portugal) for what they will fetch, for account of their owners."

It will be seen from the above extracts that the English merchants were not only aware of the *modus operandi* of manufacturing port wine as far back as 1754, but that they were in point of fact the instigators of such a nefarious practice; and if a concocted article "made to order" would command a higher price than the pure juice of the grape, we cannot consistently blame the growers for carrying out the wishes and executing the orders of their customers. It is undoubtedly an unsatisfactory state of things, but it is evident that full justice has not been done to the genuine wines of the Douro, nor has their true character been fairly developed.

Port is the produce of the province of Traz os Montes (behind the mountains), on the *alto* Douro, the higher or northern bank of that river. The scenery is described as a series of hills covered with vines, interspersed here and there with a few stray olive trees. Mrs. Baillie thus describes it :—

> " Hard by the olive and the purple vine,
>     Their mingled treasures lavishly bestow ;
> Oh ! favour'd land, thus corn, and oil, and wine,
>     Along thy happy valleys ever flow,
> And bid man's ravish'd heart in grateful warmth to
>     glow ! "—MRS. BAILLIE'S ' *Lisbon.*' (1824.)

Of the \*other wines of Portugal, the white wine known as *Lisbon* is entitled to our next consideration. It is a useful sweet wine, possessing considerable body, and from fifty to eighty years back was in very general use. We read of it being the daily custom with the merchants of that day to go to Tom's Coffee House in Cornhill, to have their luncheon gill of Lisbon and bread and cheese.

*Bucellas* is also in much repute, and has

---

\* A pipe of Port is 115 gallons; a pipe of Lisbon, Bucellas, and Calcavello 117 gallons.

been extensively used as a dinner wine; and might vie with Hock, Chablis, Sauterne, or any of the light wines for that purpose, if they would only let us have it more free from spirit.

*Termo* is a light and refreshing wine but little known here. Mrs. Baillie, who resided sometime at Lisbon, thus writes :—" We have tasted a sort of white light wine sold here, which we thought almost as refreshing and excellent as Hock; and for which the common charge is about two-pence a bottle. It is made in the vicinity of Lisbon, and is known by the name of *Vinho de Termo.*"

*Calcavello* is a sweet wine of delicious muscatel flavour, and is made near Belem.

There is likewise a red wine, known as *Colares Port*, which when pure, is of good quality.

At Villa Nova, which is on the opposite side of the river to Oporto, there are very extensive stores, or as they are called *lodges*, where many thousands of casks are stored. It is here that the process of blending the wines takes place. When the vintage wines

come in they are tasted, and separated into
one, two, or more lots; and when the entire
purchases made in the wine-country have
been received, then comes the operation of
lotting for that particular vintage. After
this, according to the orders received and
the quality required, the blending of the
different wines follows; and so much of
the finest and old matured stock is used in
proportion to the new wine as may be
warranted by the price agreed on for the
article.

The grape-blight first made its appearance on the Portuguese vines in 1853, and
appears to have reached its climax in 1856-7.
The effects of the disease in this region
were deplorable, reducing the annual crop
to one quarter of the average. It was
indeed the most disastrous event that
could happen to the wine-farmers, as they
depend for existence on their grapes, much
of the soil being too poor for other culture.

Lisbon *(Lisboa* in Portuguese) is situated
on the northern bank of the Tagus, from
which it is seen in the form of an amphi-

theatre, being built on a succession of hills, the highest of which are the hill of Buenos Ayres to the west, and the castle-hill to the east. At the mouth of the Tagus a large square tower forms a conspicuous object, and serves to defend both the suburb and the entrance of the river.

> " The lofty tower,
> Which to this very hour
> Stands looking sea-ward."

At this fort, known as Belem Castle, all the vessels which enter the port of Lisbon are first visited by the custom-house officers. Near it is a commodious quay with numerous wharves, made in the time of Joseph I. This part of Lisbon suffered least from the great earthquake of 1755, which was so destructive to other portions of the city; and this partial immunity is ascribed by Mr. Link to the fact of the place being built on a rock of basalt, which he supposes to have been forced up by a similar convulsion at some very remote period. The population of Lisbon is reckoned at 260,000 inhabitants; its trade, though much dimi-

nished since the loss of Brazil, is still considerable. The greater part of the country
round Lisbon is covered with large gardens,
called *quintas*, which are generally laid out
with orange and olive plantations, and sometimes with vineyards, and even corn fields.
Orange, olive, cypress, and judas trees, with
elms and poplars, are the trees met with in
the neighbourhood of Lisbon. Orange
trees abound both in the *quintas*, as well as
in open spaces. The fruit is perfectly ripe
in May, and continues till August. Oranges
for exportation are gathered in February,
before they are ripe.

It will be seen from the published reports
that Port wine has not suffered by the
introduction of French and other light
wines, the consumption of 186$\frac{2}{3}$ being considerably in excess of that of the previous
year. The following is the number of
gallons entered for Home Consumption
during the last seven years ; shewing, notwithstanding the admission of the lower
class wines at the shilling duty on January 1, 1861, an average increase on Port

of 780,941 gallons for the last three
years.

| | |
|---|---|
| 1857 . . . . | 2,304,886 |
| 1858 . . . . | 1,921,677 |
| 1859 . . . . | 2,020,561 |
| 1860 . . . . | 1,776,172 |
| 1861 . . . . | 2,702,707 |
| 1862 . . . . | 2,349,954 |
| 1863 . . . . | 2,618,680 |

The entire produce of wine in Portugal
is estimated at an average of about
50,000,000 gallons.

# CHAPTER XIV.

## On the Wines of Madeira, the Canaries, etc.

" In vite hominis vitam esse diceres."—Ovid.

ADEIRA is an island situated in the Atlantic Ocean, about 400 miles from the north-western coast of Africa. It is nearly 45 miles long, and its greatest breadth nearly 20 miles; the area is said to be 360 square miles. This island is one mass of basalt, rising with a steep ascent from the south and north towards the interior, the most elevated portion of the rock being from 4000 to 5000 feet. The declivities of the mountain are furrowed by deep valleys traversed by streams. These valleys contain gardens and vine-yards, but the latter are chiefly formed on the ridges and slopes of the rocks, some as high as 2500 feet above the sea. The climate of Madeira is very mild, the mean temperature of the year not exceeding 68°, and in the winter months the thermometer rarely sinks below 60°; whilst the supply of rain is even, constant, and not delayed, nor immoderate. For these reasons the island has been regarded as especially healthy, and has consequently been much resorted to by invalids from northern climes, more especially those afflicted with pulmonary complaints, who seek in its soft air and genial influence the means of diminishing their sufferings and prolonging life.

It is supposed that vineyards were first established in the island about the middle of the fifteenth century, and that the vines for that purpose were brought from Candia. The uniformity of the climate and the volcanic nature of the soil were so favourable to their development, that the wines of Madeira at a very early period obtained that reputation which they have maintained for such a length of time. The principal

K

wines are (we fear we shall ere long have to speak in the past tense) the *Sercial, Bual,* and the *Malmsey,* or as it is termed by way of distinction, *Malmsey Madeira;* the latter is a sweet wine, and besides these there is a red wine called the *Tinta.* The two former are very dry, and are the sorts with which we have been most familiarized. When new the wines of Madeira are of great body, and marked by a degree of roughness and harshness, that render them unfit for use until they are toned down and matured by age, or, what is far preferable, a long sea-voyage. Some imagine the character of the wines to have deteriorated of late years, but the fact is, that Madeira, like all other wine countries, furnished a variety of growths and qualities, and of these England only received a small portion of its choicer produce, and in most instances this was mellowed and improved by a sea voyage by way of the East or West Indies.

We find that in 1833 the shipments of Madeira were reported at from 15,000 to

16,000 pipes,* and from this time in particular may be dated the progressive diminution of supply. In the first instance the
evil may be traced to over-shipment, which
in a bad year left them no old wines to
fall back upon, consequently they were not
able to ship the required quantity or to
keep up the quality, and years of comparative scarcity following, further increased
their difficulties. This state of things was
succeeded by the *oidium* blight, which made
its appearance two years earlier than it did
on the Douro, and in a much more virulent
form, destroying the entire crop, and fatally
infecting the plant itself. The yield had
been decreasing year after year for a considerable period ; but now the vines were
nearly every where extirpated, and the few
that escaped have seldom produced healthy
fruit since ; indeed for six years there has
been little or no vintage. Many of the
proprietors of the grounds abandoned as
hopeless the future cultivation of the vine,

---

* A pipe of Madeira is 92 gallons.

and this growing indifference has led in
many instances to the vineyards being
replaced by sugar plantations. Efforts are,
however, being made by the introduction
of fresh varieties, especially the Catawba
and Isabella species, both of which are indigenous to America, and these are grafted
on the old stocks.   But from the nature of
the soil and climate, none but old vines
will produce first-class wine; it must therefore necessarily take some years before
the experiment can possibly succeed.

The consumption of Madeira, and the
per centage it bears with other wines in
this respect, is shewn as under :—

| | | | | | |
|---|---|---|---|---|---|
| In 1831 consumption | 209,127 | galls. and | 3·56 | per cent. |
| 1841 | ,, | 107,701 | ,, | 1·58 | ,, |
| 1851 | ,, | 71,025 | ,, | 1·14 | ,, |
| 1859 | ,, | 29,566 | ,, | 0·41 | ,, |
| 1860 | ,, | 28,242 | ,, | 0·39 | ,, |
| 1861 | ,, | 28,749 | ,, | 0·27 | ,, |
| 1862 | ,, | 31,906 | ,, | 0·32 | ,, |

The Canaries are a group of islands in
the North Atlantic Ocean, lying off the
coast of Africa.   This group consists of
the following large islands :—Canary, Te-

neriffe, Palma, Ferro, Gomera, Fuertaven-
tura, and Lanzarote; there are also some
smaller ones, as Santa Clara, Alegranza,
and Graciosa. The Peak of Teneriffe, a
half-extinct volcano, rises to the height of
about 11,400 feet, and as it is viewed from
the sea at a distance, seems to spring out of
the water like a sugar-loaf. The vine is
largely cultivated, and in most of the islands wine is made, which is well known
in Europe under the name of " Teneriffe,"
from the fact of that island being the principal seat of the wine trade, rather than it
being the distinctive name of any particular
wine grown in the islands.

The Canary islands have belonged to
Spain since the fourteenth century, and
constitute a province governed by a cap-
tain-general. The capital, Santa-Cruz, has
an eastern aspect with an extensive but
unprotected port. Works are now being
actively pursued in the formation of a mole,
which when completed will be of great
advantage to the shipping. The present
population is calculated at 10,900, and the
gross population of all the islands at 200,000.

The ancients designated these the Fortunate Islands, and judged by their situation, climate, and natural productions, it would scarcely appear an exaggeration, for the agricultural resources of the islands are most exuberant. Coffee, sugar, cotton, yield with little cultivation; and the fruits of the South—oranges, bananas, mangoes, and exquisite grapes, are equally plentiful; as are also figs, apples, pears, peaches, and other northern fruits; whilst the gardens abound in every species of tropical plants and flowers. Vegetation in a soil and climate so favoured is rapid and most abundant.

Of the wines grown in the Canary isles, perhaps that most known, although it has fallen much into disuse, is the wine recognised under the name of *Vidonia*, or bastard Madeira, or as it is sometimes called Teneriffe. It is a dry wine, of good body, although somewhat coarse, and derives its name from the *vidogna* grape; large quantities were formerly shipped by way of the West Indies to their various destinations, and doubtless the voyage itself, as well as the time occupied therein, would do much in mellowing and developing the better qualities of the wine. We are told that the annual consumption was formerly 30,000 pipes,* and most probably much of this passed muster as Madeira, yet at the present time there cannot be a twentieth part of this quantity consumed. The *Malmsey*, or Malvasia, is, true to the qualities of Malmsey of old, very rich and luscious, and was once greatly in request, doubtless at that early period when the word Malmsey was the general term for a sweet white wine, irrespective of what country it might be the produce. Wine of that name is also produced in Spain, as well as elsewhere ; and it would indeed be a problem at the present day to define where the wine was grown which proved so fatal to " maudlin Clarence in his Malmsey butt." From the confusion arising from a want of classification in the nomenclature of wines some two or three centuries back, considerable doubt

---

* A pipe of Vidonia (or Teneriffe) is 100 gallons.

exists as to the precise nature of many of them ; but we are led to believe that those of the Canary islands became included under the general term, Sack. The reader is referred to an article on this subject in Chapter XII, under the head of " Wines of Spain." That the consumption of Canary wines was somewhat considerable, and the quality held in high repute, is shewn on good authority. In 1617, a pipe of *Canary*, presented by the City of Bristol to the Earl of Pembroke, is reported to have cost £15. 4*s*. 8*d*., and we find that in half a century afterwards the price had more than doubled. Referring to Canary wine, we find that about the year 1662, Howell, who had been appointed by Charles II. Historiographer Royal, says, " Of this wine, if of any other, may be verified that merry induction, that good wine maketh good blood, good blood causeth good humours, good humours cause good thoughts, good thoughts bring forth good works, and good works carry a man to heaven ; *ergo*, good wine carrieth a man to heaven. If this be true, surely more English go to heaven this way than any other ; for I think there is more Canary brought into England than to all the world besides." These islands, in common with Madeira, suffered excessively from the *oidium*, as in this case also, the great age of the vines rendered them less able to withstand the disease.

In including in this chapter the productions of South America, we have been guided rather by a similarity in the nature of these wines to those we have just referred to, than by any regard to geographical proximity.

Although South America abounds in vineyards, those cultivated for the manufacture of wine may be said to be situated chiefly on that side of the coast which is bounded by the South Pacific Ocean. Chili has hitherto been regarded as producing the best wine, and the vines of Chili have been referred to by travellers as luxuriant and abundant. Of late years Peru has furnished a wine known in the English market as *Peruvian Madeira*. Without laying claim to their delicacy and softness, this wine possesses some of the flavour of Madeira wines, but whether this is the innate flavour of the Peruvian wine, or is given to it by blending the natural wine with a portion of common Madeira, we cannot undertake to say. A recent writer unhesitatingly denounces the wine in the following terms :—" I have several times carefully tasted this (so-called) wine of Peru, but have each time become more strongly convinced that the proportion of Peruvian, if any, in the casks, is very small; and that it is composed of a common clean-flavoured white wine from Spain, prepared, and re-shipped to England." The opinion we have just quoted is one entitled to considerable respect, but from written authorities we find it stated, "As early as 1825 I have known and drunk the wines of Peru ;" and again we read that "in 1860 in the valley of the Teâ alone, 10,000 barrels of wine, to imitate Sherry, Madeira, and Malaga, were made ;" and as we know these wines are shipped from Callao, we have no reasonable grounds for doubting them to be the produce of the. locality. Some samples of Peruvian wines were shewn at the International Exhibition of 1862, and the following remarks respecting them are taken from the Report of the Jurors :*—" In South America considerable attention has been paid of late years to the cultivation of the vine, and some wines are now made in Peru and adjacent districts which approach more nearly than any of the wines of Europe to some of the ordinary Madeiras of old."

---

* By Joseph Prestwich, F.R.S. (a juror.) Reprinted for private circulation by permission of the Society of Arts, by Clowes and Sons, 1863.

# CHAPTER XV.

---

## On the Wines of Germany, Hungary, Austria, and Switzerland.

> " Bright with bold wine,
> From the old Rhine,
> Take this goblet in thy hand !
> Quaff the Rhenish bumper gleely,
> Let thy true blood flow as freely
> For our German Fatherland ! "
>
> *Burschen Melody.*
>
> " For an offering meet at friendship's shrine
> Is a deep, deep draught of the good Rhine wine."
>
> *Old Song.*

---

CONSIDERABLE doubt exists as to the precise time of the introduction of the vine into western Europe, nor do we collect from any reliable authority that it can date back to a very remote period. The probability seems to be that the Germans were indebted for their first vines to their Roman conquerors. That no vineyards existed in Germany at the time of

Tacitus is manifest, for he asserts, in his description of that country, that the soil was "unpropitious to every sort of fruit tree,—the usual beverage of the people being a kind of beer made from wheat or barley." Whether in the lapse of successive ages the climate has undergone a proportionate amelioration, or what causes have operated to favour to such an extent the vineyards of the Rhine districts, we will not stop to enquire. Certain it is that the Germans have good reason to be enthusiastic in praise of their wines ; and in no wine-producing countries are vineyards cultivated with greater care than in the wine districts of Germany. It has been supposed that the Emperor Probus, as early as the third century, planted the vine on the Rhine ; which is far from being improbable, as we find that the poet Ausonius in the fourth century sang of the vine of the Moselle. Others relate that the Emperor Charles the Great, observing from his castle in Ingelheim that the snow on the Rüdesheim mountain always melted much sooner than in the country round, was induced to plant on that favoured spot vines which he had obtained for that purpose from Orleans; and the result has shewn that he could scarcely have selected a more appropriate locality.   It is stated that the vine was introduced in the Rheingau about the ninth century.   This chief wine growing district belonged in the middle ages to the Archbishop of Mentz, and the growth of wine was chiefly confined to those residing in and connected with the monasteries.   In later times the ecclesiastical estates were parcelled out and sold as crown lands, and are at present mostly occupied by tenants of small vineyards.   There are, however, in Rheingau larger estates belonging to several of the German nobility; the most valuable being those of the Duke of Nassau and Prince Metternich.

The following graphic description of the scenery of the Rhine is quoted from Mr. Cyrus Redding :—" Whoever has visited the noble Rhine, must have felt sensible of the beauty of its vineyards, covering steep and shore, interlaced with the most romantic ruins, towns, ancient and venerable, smiling villages, and the rapid broad German river, reflecting the rich scenery on its banks. Nowhere is the fondness for vine cultivation more evident in every grade and class of farmer, than in the German wine districts. The humblest peasant has his square yard of vineyard. Every accessible spot on the declivities with an auspicious aspect is decorated with the favourite plant. From Mentz even to Bonn, the vineyards of the Rhine are observed to greater advantage than any similar cultivation in other countries; Erbach, enthroned on its vines; the Rheingau, its Johannisberg on a crescent hill of red soil, adorned with cheering vegetation; every cranny cultivated that will carry the vine; Mittelheim, Geisenheim, and Rüdesheim, with its strong fine bodied wine, the grapes from which bask on their promontory of rock in the summer sun, and imbibe its generous heat from dawn to setting. Then again, on the other side, Bingen, delightful, sober, majestic, with its

terraces of vines, topped by the Château of
Klopp. The narrowed river, its steep hills
and vines, the corn and fruit which the
vicinity produces, all remind the stranger
of a second Canaan. The Bingerloch, the
ruins, and the never-failing though formal
vines scattered among them, like verdant
youth revelling amid age and decay, give a
picture nowhere else exhibited; uniting to
the joyousness of wine the sober tinge of
meditative feeling. The unclad hill-summits
back the picture, with feudal relics or monastic remains. From below Asmanns-
hausen to Lorch, crumbling ruins still mingle
with the cool leaf and rich purple of the
grape. Bacharach is near, the wine of
which, probably the fancy of the drinkers
having changed, is now pronounced second-
rate in quality, though not long ago, even
the French celebrated it in their Bacchana-
lian songs. This wine is still very good,
fashion may say what it chooses. Land-
scapes of greater beauty, joined to the luxu-
riance of fruitful vine culture, can nowhere
be seen ; perhaps there is something to be

added, for the alliance of wine and its agreeable qualities, with the noble scenery of the river. The mind will have its associations upon all subjects."

The soil found most favourable for the vine is a sort of clay of slate colour, and in this the plant flourishes exceedingly, especially on the southern slopes of hills adjoining the rivers, the vapours arising from which are said to be indispensable for maturing the grapes. In most instances the ground is covered with large stones, which tend to increase the summer heat, whilst beneath them the moisture of the earth is longer retained.

The Rheingau extends from Walluf to Lorch. The wine produced in this district is considered the best in all Germany. This is to be ascribed chiefly to the favourable situation. Here the Rhine bends itself from east to west. On the right shore are situated mountains which protect the extensive valleys and vineyards from the north winds; whilst on the opposite side of the river there are no mountains to throw their shadows across, so that the sun's rays have undiminished influence throughout the day; and in both cases the land is largely benefited by the refreshing exhalations from the Rhine.

Perhaps the most extensive of the vineyards of the Rhine is the *Rüdesheim Berg,* consisting of 400 acres. The old castle, with its lofty summit, and walls rising one above another like terraces, presents the appearance of a fortress; and the illusion is supported by the picturesque appearance in the background of the rocky mountain Ehrenfels overhanging the Bingerloche.

The far-famed *Johannisberg* appears as a single hill reclining as it were on the north of the chain of mountains in the centre of the Rheingau. This vineyard formerly belonged to the princely Abbot Fulda. It now belongs, together with the castle, which was formerly the monastery, to Prince Metternich, and is held in fief under the Emperor of Austria. There is also an estate producing fine wine called *Johannisberg Claus;* but the decided rival to the Johannisberg is the *Steinberg*, situated between Hattenheim and Erbach, formerly belonging to the Ederbach Monastery, but now the property of the Duke of Nassau. This wine possesses the same character and aroma as the Johannisberg, with greater strength. In March, 1836, the Duke of Nassau sold by auction a large portion of his old wines which had been stored for years in the Cloister of Ederbach. Such wines had never before been submitted to public sale. They comprised the choicest vintages from 1726 to 1834. There was also a cask of Steinberg, containing 3½ aums,* of the year 1822, called the Bride of the Cellar, which was knocked down to Prince Emile of Hesse Darmstadt for 6105 florins. Thus did Steinberg carry off the highest price that had ever been paid for wine. The red wines form but a very small proportion, and are chiefly those of *Assmannhausen* and *Ingelheim*. Of the other wines, the *Hinterhaus*, *Geisenheimer*, and *Marco-*

---

* An aum is 30 gallons.

*brunner* may be noted; the latter is the property of Count Schönborn. *Hochheim,* although situated on the Maine, is generally comprised among the Rhine wines, and is of excellent quality.

The wines of the Palatinate grow on the left bank of the Rhine. The principal of them are those of *Nierstein, Oppenheim, Bodenheim, Laubenheim,* and *Scharlachberg.* This district produces twice as much as the Rheingau, but not equal in quality. The wine known as *Liebfraumilch,* grown in the neighbourhood of Worms, is of very good quality.

Some good wines are grown in Rhenish Bavaria, the produce of the slopes of the Hartz mountains; but the larger proportion are devoid of any distinguishing character. The *Stein* wines, imported in bottles of a peculiar shape, termed *bocksbeutel,* are generally of fine quality, and of these the *Rieslinger* ranks the highest. At an auction sale at Wurzburg, in April of the present year, was a cask of wine 137 years old; also wines of 1783, 1789, 1807, 1811, and 1822.

The Nahe enters the Rhine at Bingen, opposite Rüdesheim, and passes through charming valleys, the greater part of which are planted with vines. The best descriptions are the *Creuznacher, Scharlachberger, Winzenheimer, Roxheimer, Norheimer, Monzinger,* &c. At Kirn a very excellent red wine is grown from Burgundy grapes planted in 1780 by Prince Dominique. Since the vineyard passed into the hands of the present proprietor, the wines have much improved in character, and that to which we have just referred, called *Kirner Schmisser,* may challenge comparison with the finer sorts of Burgundy and Claret.

In Prussia there are 60,250 *morgens** of vineyards, 22,200 of which are situated on the Moselle, and about 1200 on the Saar and the other branch rivers. Red grapes are but little grown in the Moselle, and are rarely applied to the purpose of wine making; those required for the effervescent wines are the produce of the Palatinate.

---

* A morgen is about an English acre.

The quantity of wine produced in Prussia
varies in different seasons from 65,000 to
200,000 aums, about three-fifths of which
are grown on the Moselle.  From Treves
up the Moselle, on the so-called Upper
Moselle, is grown the more ordinary descriptions of *Moselle;* and of these the
inferior sorts are largely shipped to France,
and converted into red wines ; whilst much
of the better quality is sent to the Prussian
provinces on the Baltic, to be used in the
manufacture of Champagne.  From Treves
down to Coblentz is called the Lower
Moselle, and it is there that the finer wines
are grown.  They are known as *Oligsberger*,
*Neuberger*, *Josephshöfer*, *Brauneberger*, *Zel-
tinger*, &c.  On the Saar are also produced
some excellent wines, the best of which are
the *Scharzhofberger*, *Bochsteimèr*, *Canzener*,
*Wiltinger*, &c.

The manufacture of sparkling wines in
Germany is of comparatively recent date ;
and as the Germans had been amongst the
largest consumers of Champagne, and were
in a position to produce a similar article at

a much less cost, we need look for no other reason for their taking up this branch of industry. *Sparkling Hock*, as well as *sparkling Moselle*, varies considerably in quality ; the finer descriptions being excellent, whilst the commoner sorts are almost worthless. The German effervescent wines are made from the wines of the Palatinate, these being peculiarly adapted for the purpose. We have stated elsewhere that a particular flavouring is added to all sparkling wines ; as regards Moselle a fresh ingredient is introduced,—the flowers of the elder, *Sambucus niger*, which contribute to impart to the wine the aroma by which Moselle is so readily distinguished. The sparkling wines are principally made at Hochheim, Mayence, Frankfort, and Coblentz.

The Tyrol is a princely county of Germany in the circle of Austria. The quality of its wine is by no means commensurate with the quantity of grapes, which abound in great profusion. The wines are thin and delicate, and deficient in tone, body, and keeping properties.

The wines of Germany are distinguished by their great freedom from alcohol, and therefore their extreme durability cannot be owing to the amount of spirit which they possess. Professor Liebig attributes their distinctive character to the free acid which they contain, and is of opinion that it is to this cause they derive their valuable hygienic properties. In calcareous complaints the light and pure wines of Germany have been resorted to with extraordinary benefit,* and the fact of these diseases being scarcely known amongst the inhabitants is quoted as a proof of the singular advantage the wines possess in this respect.† Throughout the states of Germany scarcely any other wine is used but

---

* Dr. Prout. 'On Stomach and Renal Diseases.' 4th edit. p. 210.

† Doubtless this is true, inasmuch as the German wines are known to possess lithontriptic properties, probably from the free acid referred to by Liebig, as well as from the phosphorus, which, according to Kletzinsky, is inherent in the wines of western Europe. But a different reason may be assigned for these diseases being so comparatively rare. The foolish practice is unknown there of

that produced in the country, and the Germans are not only proud of extolling the excellence of their wines, but also ascribe to them many curative properties ; and the proverb that " good Hock keeps off the doctor" is not only a familiar one, but also "as old as the hills."

The following is from the Report of the Jurors on the Wines of the International Exhibition of 1862 :—"Celebrated for many ages, and holding deservedly a first rank in the.wine-growing countries of Europe, the wines of the Rhine have of late years especially been much used in England, where they have to a certain extent supplanted the white wines of France. These wines vary exceedingly in body, and considerably in flavour, but they are essentially class wines. Those of the Moselle mostly possess a muscatel flavour, which is often heightened by artificial means. Compara-

---

mothers continually dosing their children with magnesia, which, being insoluble, forms dangerous concretions in the bowels, and lays the train for the formation, in after life, of stone and calculus.

tively little red wine is made. Some years since the manufacture of sparkling wines was introduced ; and in the Moselle district it has now become an important trade, so rapidly has the taste for these wines spread. The smaller states of Germany produce some very good wines, many of which compete with the general run of Rhine wines. They are worth attention ; but the exhibition of them on this occasion has been of a very scanty description. The produce of the Zollverein may be estimated at 2,000,000 gallons."

Hungary, as a wine-producing country, has hitherto been but little known ; but the soil and climate are admirably adapted for the successful cultivation of the grape. The delay and cost of transit have been serious obstacles to the shipment of these wines, as may be seen by reference to the relative position of Pesth and the usual shipping ports, Hamburg and Bremen. By Trieste the expense is less, but a long sea voyage is involved, which has been found too severe a test for some of the lower class wines. The produce is very considerable, and the demand so far short, that it is no unusual occurrence for the growers to have stored in their cellars some thousands of eimers* waiting for purchasers.

*Tokay*, imperial Tokay, formerly the only wine known in England as the produce of Hungary, is thick, luscious, and full of flavour. It requires great age, and we are told that it is only in perfection when a century old. It has, for a length of time, enjoyed a world-wide reputation, but is now rarely met with; and we question whether the merits of the wine are at all in proportion to the "fancy price" it is sold at. Dr. Henderson, quoting from Ritter's 'Weinlehre,' says of Tokay :—"When the Emperor of Austria wished to make a present of some Tokay wine, in return for a breed of horses which had been sent to him by the ex-King of Holland, the stock in the

---

* An eimer is 11. 8 gallons.

imperial and royal cellars was not deemed sufficiently old for the purpose, and 2,000 bottles of old Tokay were therefore procured from Cracow, at the extravagant price of seven ducats* per bottle."

Hungary contains more than a hundred different sorts of wine. After Tokay, the best white wines are those of *St. George, Odenburg,* and the *Carlowitz.* The most celebrated of the red wines are the *Menes, Buda, Erlauer, Ofner,* and the *Gros Wardein.*

Hitherto wine has not been grown with a view to exportation. The Hungarians, primitive, simple, and poor, are satisfied with what they can get with little trouble, and content to live from hand to mouth. " Many of the Hungarian wines," remarks Mr. Graham Dunlop,† in his official report, "are agreeable and wholesome when drunk

---

* The ducat is equivalent to about 9*s.* 5*d.* sterling.

† British Secretary of Legation at Vienna. See *Parliamentary Report,—Secretaries of Embassies,* 1862.

on the spot, but they are in general made with a view merely to home or neighbouring markets, and with little or no regard to foreign consumption, or to their fitness for undergoing transport. Consequently, although the people thoroughly understand the culture and management of the grape until the vintage, their whole system of wine making and manipulation is careless, wasteful, and defective, and requires improvement."

The following is from the Report of the Jurors on the Wines of the International Exhibition of 1862 :—" Great expectations have been formed of the capabilities of Hungary as a wine supplying country. The produce is large, amounting to nearly 250,000,000 gallons per annum; a large quantity of which is exported to Russia and Poland, and small quantities have of late found their way to England. Many of the wines are good, but more careful treatment is generally required. The celebrated wine of Tokay is better known by name than by experience, and, from its expensive character, is not likely to become an object of trade."   .

The wines of Austria are at present but little known in this country, and it was not until the Exhibition of 1862 that we had a fair opportunity of judging of their merits. In referring either to Austrian or Hungarian wines, it is frequently the practice to confuse one with the other, and indeed to confound together the general produce of the Austrian dominions. The wines are, however, so dissimilar, that we must clearly be understood as referring now to those grown in Austria *proper.*

These wines possess a high character, and although remarkably free from spirit, are so perfectly fermented as to bear a long sea voyage without the slightest detriment. We have tasted samples which were on board the 'Novara' frigate during a three years' scientific expedition; and they were not only uninjured, but on the contrary greatly improved. The finest wines we

have seen are those of *Vöslau, Goldeck,*
and *Steinberg;* of each of which there is a
red and white variety. The red wines of
Austria may challenge comparison with any
of the Bourdeaux wines of a much higher
price; they are fuller in body, and consequently better adapted for consumption in
this country. The vines employed are
those of Portugal, and the wine itself may
be said to bear some resemblance both to
Port and Burgundy, and in this respect is
well suited to English tastes. The effervescent description, *Sparkling Vöslauer,* is
an agreeable wine, with considerable flavour
and fine aroma.

The vineyards which produce these wines
are situated to the south of Vienna, and
lie between the Hungarian mountains and
the slopes of the Styrian Alps; and the
Vienna and Trieste railway being closely
adjacent, offers ready facilities of transit.
The soil and climate are so well adapted to
the growth of the grape, and the wines so
delicious in quality, that we make no doubt

the Austrian produce only requires to be known. In all cases it takes some little time before a really good article can obtain a chance of being acknowledged, so difficult is it to divert the stream of demand from its ordinary channel; but we venture to predict that ere many years elapse these wines will in their turn to a great extent take the place of other wines now in use.

The following paragraph appeared in the money article of the 'Times,' of January 4, 1864 :—" The chief disappointment with regard to the effect of the reduced duties has been felt by the producers of those countries whose wines had been little previously known, but who expected that they would then come into notice. The Austrian growers especially complain that many qualities, which our merchants admit to be unexceptionable, are left even without a trial by the English public, owing to the indisposition of the dealers to depart from their routine channels, and the absence of any tendency to judge for themselves on the part of the great proportion of English consumers."

The following is from the ' Daily Telegraph,' of September 26, 1862, and forms part of an article headed "International Exhibition :"—"Almost the only wine of any note which is comparatively strange to Englishmen, and is likely to become an established favourite among them, is in the Austrian department, being the singularly pure, generous, and fragrant produce of the vineyards of Austria, exhibited by Mr. R. Schlumberger, a juror of Class 3. The qualities of a really fine Burgundy wine are here assimilated with a distinct and original character, which the true judge will quickly discern and appreciate."

The following is taken from the Report of the Jurors on the Wines of the International Exhibition of 1862 :—"The vine is largely cultivated in many parts of Austria, and the average yield of wine may be estimated at about 200,000,000 gallons. This includes many wines of good quality and of good keeping properties."

M

The following is given as the total quantity of wine grown throughout the Austrian dominions, estimated in gallons.

| | | |
|---|---:|---:|
| Austria *Proper* . . . . | 40,000,000 | |
| Moravia and Bohemia . . | 12,500,000 | |
| | | 52,500,000 |
| Styria . . . . . . . | 21,000,000 | |
| Carniola and Tyrol . . . | 14,000,000 | |
| | | 35,000,000 |
| Istria, Trieste . . . . | 15,000,000 | |
| Dalmatia . . . . . . | 17,500,000 | |
| Lombardy, Venetian Kingdom | 45,000,000 | |
| | | 77,500,000 |
| Croatia and bordering districts | 110,000,000 | |
| Hungary . . . . . . | 210,000,000 | |
| Transylvania . . . . . | 18,000,000 | |
| | | 338,000,000 |
| Total | | 503,000,000 |

Switzerland, from its geographical position, and its icy glaciers and perpetual peaks of snow, can scarcely be supposed to possess any natural claims to be recognized as a wine growing country. Nevertheless it produces several good wines. The best are the red wines of *Salquener*, and of *Neufchâtel;* and the white of *Chiavenna*, and of *Yvorne*. The growths of the *Valteline* are also of good quality and of great durability.

The Report of the Jurors on the Wines of the International Exhibition of 1862 states : — " Switzerland produces about 7,000,000 gallons of wine per annum ; this, however, is scarcely sufficient for its consumption, and a considerable quantity is imported from France. Some of the Swiss wines are agreeable and keep well. Of late years the manufacture of sparkling wines has been introduced with much success. With the exception of a few of these the wines of Switzerland are hardly known in England."

# CHAPTER XVI.

## On the Wines of Italy, Sicily, and Sardinia.

" Far to the right, where Appennine ascends,
Bright as the summer, Italy extends;
Her uplands sloping deck the mountain's side,
Woods over woods in gay theatric pride ;
While oft some temple's mould'ring top between
With venerable grandeur marks the scene."
Goldsmith. ' *The Traveller.*'

s we have already referred at some length to the vines and vineyards of Italy (Chapter VI.), we shall, in the present instance, confine ourselves to a brief description of its vinous products.

Next to the growth of cereals, wine is the most important production of the soil of Italy. The wines of modern Italy are numerous, and vary in quality; yet, notwithstanding the advantage of climate and soil, they have not maintained the character which they possessed in the earlier ages; and we look in vain for the nectar of which Anacreon sung of yore, or the *Cæcuban* and *Falernian* wines which graced the symposia of the imperial Cæsars, and were immortalized by Horace and Virgil. The farfamed Falernian was grown about the bases of hills, and Galen observes that there were two sorts, the dry and the sweetish; he states that the latter was only produced when the wind continued in the south during the vintage. Martial dignifies Falernian with the epithet " immortal ":—

" Addere quid cessas, puer, immortale Falernum ?"
‘ *Epigrammata*,’ ix. 94.

But, although the name of Falernian be familiar with us as " household words," nothing is known of its taste, flavour, or colour. It is, however, described as a strong wine, that would keep long, and so rough that it required to be cellared a great number of years before it was sufficiently mellowed.

Throughout the whole extent of the country vines are grown and wine made; but as there is little or no external demand, the wine, although abundant, is almost entirely grown for home consumption; so that but little stimulus is offered to competition in respect to the quality of the wine produced.

Italy produces the *Vino Greco*, which is a rich gold coloured wine, and is grown near Mount Vesuvius. In the same neighbourhood is made the *Mangiaguerra*, and also a thick blackish wine called *Verrachia;* and at the base of the hill the delicious *Vino vergine*. The kingdom of Naples affords the *Pausillipo, Muscatel, Salernitan,* and other excellent wines; and also the *Chiarello*, which is much drunk in Rome. But the most prized is the rich luscious wine known as *Lachrymæ Christi*, supposed by some to be the Falernian of the Romans. The Papal States produce the pleasant *Albano* and *Orvieto*, and the sweet *Montefiascone*. In Tuscany are produced the white and red *Florence*, and also the rich

*Montepulciano*, described by Francisco Redi, in his poem of ' Bacco in Toscana,' as " the king of all wine." Of the Tuscan wines, Leigh Hunt says, in the notes to his translation of ' Bacco in Toscana': " The vines of the south seem as if they were meant to supply the waste of animal spirits occasioned by the vivacity of the natives. Tuscany is one large vineyard and olive ground. What would be fields and common hedges in England, are here a mass of orchards, producing wine and oil, so that the sight becomes tiresome in its very beauty." In Lombardy are produced the *Modenese* and *Montserrat*. The finest *Muscadine* is grown between Nizza and Savona; this wine is said to have been kept upwards of two hundred years, and is held in much repute. The *Vino d'Asti* of Piedmont is also a wine much used.

To give some idea of the vast capabilities of Italy as a wine-growing country, statists have declared that, taking the quantity of wine made at only 14*s.* per hectolitre, the total value of this product would amount to nearly twenty-three million pounds

sterling. Were there only a little more
attention paid to the choice of the vines
best fitted for cultivation, and were the
grapes best suited for each particular wine
more carefully gathered and selected, a
great step would be gained towards the
production of better wines; and were both
the progress of pressing the grapes and the
fermentation of the juice better attended
to, or, in short, were the Italians only to
imitate the best methods so successfully
followed in France, Germany, Portugal,
and Spain, the produce of the Italian vineyards would not only be vastly increased,
but the quality of wines would be greatly
improved, and their value prodigiously enhanced. But in countries where wine is so
abundant that all may drink it, little money
value is attached to it, and it consequently
becomes neglected.

The grape disease, so devastating to all
wine countries, did not make its appearance
in these parts till a much later period, and
its effects were comparatively trifling.

The wines of Sicily are few in number,
and not distinguished by any particular

excellence of quality. The principal of these is *Marsala*, or *Bronti*, as it was formerly called, from having been grown on an estate of that name, belonging to Lord Nelson, who numbered amongst his titles that of Duke of Bronti. The town of Marsala, from whence the wine takes its name, is situated on the promontory of Lilybæum, at the west corner of Sicily; where Garibaldi landed on his memorable expedition in May, 1860. The necessity for a wine of moderate price, obtained for Marsala, on its introduction some fifty years ago, a considerable demand, but it will be seen by the following statement of consumption and per centage to other wines, that Marsala* is gradually falling into disuse :—

In 1831 consumption 259,916 galls. and 4·18 per cent.
   1841     ,,     401,439    ,,    6·49   ,,
   1851     ,,     394,225    ,,    6·28   ,,
   1859     ,,     227,657    ,,    3·13   ,,
   1860     ,,     209,154    ,,    2·84   ,,
   1861     ,,     231,270    ,,    2·13   ,,
   1862     ,,     214,125    ,,    2·18   ,,

* A pipe of Marsala is 93 gallons.

Sicily also produces a red wine, some-what resembling claret, called *Lissa;* it is not remarkable for any distinguishing merit, and is but little known.

Sardinia produces a considerable quantity of wine, of good quality, and such is the abundance of the grapes, that were it not for the indolent apathy of the people, there is little doubt but that ten times the quantity of wine might be made, and that these wines would have a reputation and a demand beyond their own locality. Among these the amber-coloured *Nasco*, and *Giro*, a red variety, are the most worthy of remark.

The following is taken from the report of the Jurors on the Wines of the International Exhibition of 1862 : " The annual produce of Italy, including Sicily and Sardinia, amounts to about 350,000,000 gallons. An infinite variety of vines are grown, but the produce of the greater number of vineyards is of common quality, little attention being shewn either in the selection of the grapes, or in the mode of making and

preserving the wine. Consequently there
are but few of the wines of Italy which can
be exported, or which take a high rank.
Amongst the best are those of Aliatico,
Asti, Orvieto, Montepulciano, and Lachrymæ Christi. That by care and attention
greater firmness and soundness can be attained, is evident from the results obtained
in Sicily, where the wine of Marsala, which
was unknown in this country till the end of
the last century, attained in 1855 a consumption of 295,304 gallons. The cha-
racteristics of the Italian wines are astrin-
gency and sweetness, combined in some
cases with considerable delicacy and flavour,
which render them extremely pleasant and
agreeable in the places of production, but
they are generally wanting in that firmness
and perfect fermentation which would fit
them for exportation to distant countries.
With the exception of Marsala, the Italian
wines are almost unknown in England.
Some of these wines possess considerable
body, containing from 20 to 28 per cent. of

proof spirit. Some of the wines of the island of Sardinia, especially the Muscat wines, are esteemed, and are exported to the north of Europe; but at present Sardinia, like Italy, has had to import wines."

# CHAPTER XVII.

On the Wines of Greece, Ionian Islands, Persia, Turkish Provinces, and the Crimea.

" The isles of Greece, the isles of Greece !
Where burning Sappho lov'd and sung,
Where grew the arts of war and peace,—
Where Delos rose, and Phœbus sprung !
Eternal summer gilds them yet,
But all, except their sun is set.

The mountains look on Marathon—
And Marathon looks on the sea ;
And musing there an hour alone,
I dream'd that Greece might still be free;
For standing on the Persians' grave,
I could not deem myself a slave.

Fill high the bowl with Samian wine !
Our virgins dance beneath the shade—
I see their glorious black eyes shine ;
But gazing on each glowing maid,
My own the burning tear-drop laves,
To think such breasts must suckle slaves."
BYRON. '*Don Juan,*' *canto* iii. *st.* 86, *v.* 1-3-11.

AMONG the wines in use at the present day, those of Greece and the islands of the Archipelago may be considered as the earliest known. Chios, now called Scio, has from the most remote period held a high reputation for its wine. Pliny praises emphatically the luscious Chian wine, and Strabo pronounces it to be the best in all Greece. Homer gave this island the appellation of " fertile," and a wine known as *Homer's Nectar*, is produced there at the present day.

The island of Candia, formerly called Crete, has also been renowned for the quantity and excellence of its wines, particularly that spoken of by Diodorus, as *Pramnian* wine, and Martial speaks of a white luscious sort, called *Passum*, made from dried grapes. This island was also celebrated for its *Malmsey*, or *Malvasia*, which we are informed was first made at Napoli di Malvasia, in the Morea, although afterwards imitated in nearly every wine country in the world. It is the sweet white wine so largely imported into England from the Greek islands and elsewhere during the middle ages, under the general term of Malmsey. It was to this wine that the Italian proverb referred,—" Manna to the mouth, and balsam to the brain." Frederica Bremer, referring to it, says, " This Malvasia wine is an earthly nectar." When subject to Venetian rule, Candia and Cyprus supplied the whole of Europe with their finest dessert wines ; and so abundant was the vintage, that the former island alone is said to have exported no less than 200,000 casks of Malmsey annually. Candia still produces excellent wines. In Cyprus several varieties of red and white wine are grown, which are exported to Venice, the Black Sea, as well as to Turkey and Russia. A choice sweet wine is the produce of a domain called the Commanderia, from its having formerly belonged to the military order of the Knights of Malta, who, in 1291, on the taking of Acre by the Mussulmans, withdrew to Cyprus, where the town of Limosso was assigned to the Hospitallers as a refuge. The wine of Cyprus is very thick and luscious, and its age may be known by pouring it into a glass, and observing whether particles similar to oil adhere to the sides ; the more tenacity the wine possesses, the greater the age. Pliny states that the staircase of the celebrated temple of Diana, at Ephesus, was formed from a single vine stem of Cyprus.

Among the earliest of the Greek wines of which we have any distinct account is the *Maronean*, which Dr. Henderson imagines to have been the production of Ismaurus,* near the mouth of the Hebrus, where Ulysses received the supply which he carried with him to the land of the Cyclops. It was a black sweet wine, and from the manner that Homer sings its virtues, the quality must have been indeed superb. The *Pramnian* was a red, but not sweet wine, of equal antiquity. It was of considerable body and strength, and is said to have somewhat resembled port. It was, however, in the luscious sweet wines that the Greeks surpassed their neighbours.

Of the islands of the Archipelago, San-

---

* ' *Odyssey,*' *book* ix.

torin, formerly called Thera, originally
Calliste, is the most luxuriant. The whole
island is an entire vineyard. The chief
wines of commerce derive their names from
local affinities. The best red growth is
called *Santorin;* it partakes of the nature
of both port and claret, and is much esteemed. *Thera* is a white variety, mellow,
pleasant, and full-bodied, and is likewise
held in much repute. Another white description, called in the island the *"wine of
Night,"* is supplied of two qualities, under
the distinctive names of *Calliste* and *St. Elie,*
the former being the stouter and richer of
the two. There is also a delicious muscadine wine called *Vino Santo,* of two
varieties, the one a deep purple, the other
a golden amber; both are surpassing rich,
and diffuse a fragrant aroma. There is
also a wine called " *wine of Bacchus,*" of a
deep gold colour, which is much prized.
Frederica Bremer, in her recent book on
" Greece and the Greeks," says, " Bacchus-
wine, Santo-wine, Night-wine, Calista-wine,

and other kinds,—all good ; but the wine
of Bacchus, nevertheless, the best."

Cos, now called Zea, was celebrated
throughout Greece for the excellence of its
wines, and it was here that Hippocrates
compiled his system of medicine. Tradition
informs us that it was also in this island
that St. John wrote his inspired book of
the Revelation. Samos, noted as being
the birth-place of Pythagoras, and still
more so as the seat of the renowned Samian
pottery, produces great quantities of grapes,
which are made into red and white wine.
We are told that the wine itself was considered by the ancients as scarcely equal
to the produce of some of the other islands,
but we can hardly imagine an inferiority
in that particular wine which Byron has
chosen to celebrate above all others :—

> " Fill high the bowl with Samian wine !
> Leave battles to the Turkish hordes,
> And shed the blood of Scio's vine ! "
>         ‘ *Don Juan,*’ *canto* iii. *st.* 86, *v.* 9.

The isle of Rhodes possesses some excellent wines, nearly all of the sweet and

luscious class. Both Pliny and Galen speak
of them approvingly; and Virgil writes,
that at the banquets of the gods they were
assigned a distinguished place at the dessert,
or second course of the celestial feast :—

> "The Rhodian, sacred to the solemn day :—
> In second services is pour'd to Jove,
> And best accepted by the gods above."
>     *' Georgics,' book* ii. 143.

The isles of the Ionian Sea, once known
as the Republic of the Seven Islands,
although producing some excellent wines,
are more celebrated for the production of
the article we are so familiarized with
in our domestic relations—the dried currant. This extensive article of import
may be said to be the staple of modern
Greek commerce; it is the produce of a
vine which bears a close affinity and resemblance to the ordinary grape plant. A
stout pleasant wine called *Corinthe* is obtained from its fruit. Ithaca produces
delicious wines, " as luscious as the bee's
nectareous dew," and is ranked as the head
of the seven Ionian islands, if not of all

Greece, for its wine. The red wine of *Ithaca* is the most known, and is described as of the Hermitage flavour. Corfu, Cephalonia and Zante also produce good wines.

The Greeks possessed a greater variety of wine, and are said to have been more given to its unrestrained use, than the Romans. The principal wine makers at the dawn of our era were the monks; and it is related that frequently a party would gather round a good sized cask, and not rise from their potations till it was emptied. The eccentric Tom D'Urfey, of humorous memory, writes :—

> " Troy had a breed of stout bold men,
> But still the Greeks defied 'em,
> 'Cause each Greek drank as much as ten,
> And thus did override 'em."

The Morea, and the innumerable islands of the Ægean Sea, produce immense quantities of wine, principally red; but, unfortunately, the manipulation is directed to preserve an exquisitely luscious sweetness, rather than to render the wine delicate and fine by proper fermentation.

That the modern wines of Greece are very different to those which have been traditionally handed down to us from the earliest ages there can be but little doubt, but who will say how this degeneracy has been brought about? Doubtless, the mountain valleys and rural homes are, to some extent, tilled and occupied by a race of men in whose veins flow the same blood which animated the Spartan heroes who fell at Thermopylæ. What influences of soil, climate, culture, or other mysterious causes, can have combined to depreciate the produce, break the power, dwindle the genius, and change altogether the type of this singularly gifted race? A writer* states, in a recently published and well-written volume,—" We know, indeed, that fatal political dissensions weakened the Grecian communities within, and that successive hordes of conquerors plundered and wasted the country, and expelled the inhabitants. We know that Roman, Scla-

---

* ' The Races of the Old World,' by C. L. Brace.

vonian, Teuton, Arab, and Turk, have
either desolated Greece, or mingled their
blood with that of its ancient race. We
find still further, that these successive
devastations have at length affected the
climate and productions, and the Greece
of modern days is not at all the woody,
salubrious, well-watered, genial country,
pictured as the Greece of old. The forests
have been burned, or turned into sheep
pastures, and the encroaching desert climate
continually drives the woods higher up the
mountains. The want of wood on the arid
and calcareous soil has increased the heat
and dryness of the air; the springs have
become scanty, and the parched earth draws
no moisture from the atmosphere. The
deficiency in wood and water has obstructed
most kinds of manufactures and tillage, and
this again has reacted on the people. Still,
with all these obvious causes of the degeneracy of the Greeks, the astonishing change
in the intellectual capacity of the race is
not sufficiently accounted for, and, perhaps,
from the subtle nature of the causes at
work, never can be."

Persia is claimed as being the native seat of the grape. We cannot pretend to offer an opinion on a point so involved in obscurity; but varieties of the grape have been found indigenous in Persia which have not been met with elsewhere. There are a stoneless variety termed the *kismish*, and a black description of grape called the *samarcand;* there is also a grape known as the *damas*, from which the finest red wine is made. The kismish grapes are described by Sir R. Ker Porter as growing at Shiraz to a large size, and are in great request, both for the table and for wine purposes. On the statement of another traveller, M. Morier, even the grapes of Shiraz, in their turn, are surpassed in quality by those of Casvin. That the wines of Persia were at one time well known, and more or less used throughout Asia, there can be but little doubt, but beyond one or two varieties which have reached us, they are compara- tively unknown. The white wine of *Shiraz* is extolled both by Chardin and Kæmpfer, the latter placing it, in point of flavour and

aroma, with the best of the wines of France.
The natural obstacles which have opposed
themselves to commercial enterprise have
likewise stood in the way of wine growing
on an extensive scale, and the culture of
the vine at the present day is comparatively
neglected. Teheran, Yezd, Shamaki, Gilan,
Casvin, Tabriz, and Ispahan constitute the
principal wine districts; but the wines in-
dividually are not much known beyond
their several localities.

In ancient times, some of the celebrated
kinds of wine came from the neighbourhood of Smyrna, and the island of Tenedos
was also celebrated for its red and white
muscadine wines. Much of the wine used
in Constantinople is said to be grown on
the island of Tenedos and the adjacent
plains of Troy.

Syria possesses some of the finest valleys
in the world, between mountains whose
sides are well adapted to the cultivation of
the vine; and the variety of grape known
as the Syrian has from the earliest ages
been distinguished for its size. Schutze

says that a bunch will furnish a supper for a whole family. Syria produces red and white wines. At Damascus the "wine of Tyre" of the Scriptures, called by Ezekiel "wine of Helbon," is yet made; it is a sweet wine. There are several varieties of wine grown here, all more or less sweet, delicate, and fragrant.

The Crimea is pronounced by all writers to be singularly favourable, both in climate and soil, for the development of the vine. The first vineyards were planted in 1804, at the suggestion of the celebrated naturalist, Pallas; and French vine-dressers and farmers were engaged to cultivate and manage them. On the southern coast there are three estates, belonging to Prince Woronzow, known as *Massandra*, *Aidanil*, and *Aloupka*, which produce both red and white wine of the highest quality and *bouquet*. The annual produce of these three vineyards is stated to be about 10,000 gallons. There is also a red wine called *Koborn*, of which we are told that 600,000

vedros* were produced in the Crimea in
1831. We are informed by many who
drank the wines during the late war that
they are of excellent quality. Prior to the
occupation of the Crimea by the allied
armies, the vineyards were on the increase;
and when the country shall have recovered
from the devastating effects of that struggle,
we may probably hear of the wines of the
Crimea being not only known, but extensively appreciated.

The following is the report of the Jurors
on the Wines of the International Exhibition of 1862 on the wines of Greece, &c. :—
" From these parts of Europe we cannot at
present look for any considerable supplies.
The Ionian islands may enter into the
trade to a small extent. Greek wines are
improving, but could not yet compete with
others. Some of the islands of the Mediterranean produce stout useful wines ; and
there are cheap red wines in some of the

---

* A vedro is about 14 gallons.

Turkish provinces.   The Crimea possesses some excellent wines; but it is there, at present, almost entirely a mere fancy produce of rich proprietors.   Wines have been received in this country shipped from Odessa, but owing to the very small size of the bottles of one speculative shipment to this market some years since, and the consequent difficulty of sale here and attendant loss, there was no encouragement either to the merchant abroad or the merchant here to repeat the operation."

# CHAPTER XVIII.

## On the Wines of America and California.

" Whenever an American requests to see me (which is not unfrequently), I comply, firstly, because I respect a people who acquired their freedom by their firmness without excess; and, secondly, because these trans-Atlantic visits, ' few and far between,' make me feel as if talking with posterity from the other side of the Styx."

*'Lord Byron's Letters to Thomas Moore.'*
*(Ravenna, July 5, 1821.)*

HE wines of America are seldom heard of and rarely met with in this country, nor is there much chance, until a return to a peaceful state of things, of our better acquaintance with them. They are but few in number, and are not recognized by any distinguishing excellence of quality; and it is to the fact of their being so little known, more than to any intrinsic merit they possess, that we feel justified in devoting a chapter to the subject.

Several species of the vine are indigenous to the continent of America, and its culture was an object of early solicitude to the first colonists of North America. The vine formed a feature in the scenery of the Delaware in 1648 ; and we are told that in the year 1683 William Penn planted a vineyard in the vicinity of Philadelphia. The general climate of America is unfavourable to vine-culture, arising from the low winter temperature and the humidity of both soil and atmosphere.

Vineyards have multiplied exceedingly within the last few years, especially on the banks of the Ohio, as well as in the western states, and there is every prospect of a gradual expansion. Whether American growths will ever become an important article of export must depend mainly on the price at which they can be shipped ; and the competition in the home market, as well as the difficulty of turning the current of trade, present serious obstacles to the attainment of such a result. In the States, however, the native wines are fast supplanting the foreign ones, and at the hotels the majority of the wines are also of home produce.

The wine in most general use in America is that grown in Carolina and other Southern States, and known by the name of *Scuppernong;* it is a very light wine, somewhat resembling Rhenish, but sweeter. In the State of New York is produced the wine called *Isabella.* In Ohio, Virginia, and Missouri is grown the *Catawba.* This wine is of the same light class as the others, but it has a peculiar musky *bouquet,* and more body; it is very much esteemed, selling at prices that would be deemed exorbitant in the wine-countries of Europe. The distinguishing characteristic in all these wines is their great freedom from alcohol, containing, in fact, the smallest per centage of spirit of any wine in the world. Large quantities of sparkling wine are made at Cincinnati and St. Louis under the name of "Sparkling Catawba," which Brother Jonathan does not hesitate to affirm is superior to Champagne and all other effervescent wines. If we do not entirely agree with him in this opinion, we must, at least, admire the spirit of nationality which gives rise to it. Those who may be sceptical on the point, had better judge for themselves,—that is, if they can succeed in obtaining the wines. In the meantime we place before our readers the following beautiful lines on the subject, written by that great poet whom America may well be proud to call her own.

### CATAWBA WINE.

" This song of wine
Is a song of the vine,
To be sung by the glowing embers
Of wayside inns,
When the rain begins
To darken the drear Novembers.

It is not a song
Of the Scuppernong
From warm Carolinian valleys,
Nor the Isabel
And the Muscadel
That bask in our garden alleys :

Nor the red Mustang,
Whose clusters hang
O'er the waves of the Colorado,
And the fiery flood
Of whose purple blood
Has a dash of Spanish bravado.

For the richest and best
Is the wine of the West,
That grows by the Beautiful River;
Whose sweet perfume
Fills all the room
With a benison on the giver.

And as hollow trees
Are the haunts of bees
For ever going and coming,
So this crystal hive
Is all alive
With a swarming and buzzing and humming.

Very good in its way
Is the Verzenay,
Or the Sillery soft and creamy;
But Catawba wine
Has a taste more divine,
More dulcet, delicious, and dreamy.

There grows no vine
By the haunted Rhine,
By Danube or Guadalquiver,
Nor an island or cape,
That bears such a grape
As grows by the Beautiful River.

Drugged is their juice
For foreign use,
When shipped o'er the reeling Atlantic,
To rack our brains
With the fever pains
That have driven the Old World frantic.

To the sewers and sinks
With all such drinks,

And after them tumble the mixer;
  For a poison malign
  Is such Borgia wine,
Or at best but a Devil's Elixir.

  While pure as a spring
  Is the wine I sing,
And to praise it, one needs but name it;
  For Catawba wine
  Has need of no sign,
No tavern bush to proclaim it.

  And this song of the vine,
  This greeting of mine,
The winds and the birds shall deliver
  To the Queen of the West,
  In her garlands dressed,
On the banks of the Beautiful River."

LONGFELLOW.

The climate of California is better suited
for the growth and development of the vine.
We are told that the European plant was
first introduced by the Spaniards as early
as 1572; but it is certain that a small species
of grape, indigenous to the locality, was
plentifully met with long previous to that
time. Laudonnière, in describing his voyage
to Florida in 1562, says that, " the trees are
environed about with vines bearing grapes,
so that the number would suffice to make
the place habitable." The celebrated naval

O

commander, Sir John Hawkins, as far back as 1564, speaks of wine of an agreeable flavour, the produce of a native grape, and which was made in large quantities. The growths are known under the names of *Angelico*, *Alisa*, *Porta*, &c.; and the character of the wines is very satisfactory. We understand that a wealthy German company have established themselves about twenty miles from Angelos, and in one year have planted half a million of vines; added to which large districts are brought into culti-- vation every year. We may fairly presume, from the activity which has prevailed in this branch of industry, that the wines of California will ere long be better known throughout Europe. From a San Francisco paper of recent date we learn that California will make 1,500,000 gallons of wine this year.

# CHAPTER XIX.

## On the Wines of the British Colonies and Settlements.

"As cold waters to a thirsty soul, so is good news from a far country."—*Proverbs* xxv, 25.

---

HE Cape of Good Hope, one of the most southern points of Africa, was discovered by Bartholomew Diaz, the Portuguese navigator, in 1493, and he gave it the name of Cabo Tormentoso, or Cape of Storms. It was afterwards called the Cape of Good Hope, as an omen that the Portuguese had now a fair prospect of reaching India, the great object of their maritime expeditions. It became a Dutch settlement about the middle of the seventeenth century, and continued so until 1795, when

it was taken by the English. At the peace
of Amiens it was restored to the Dutch, but
was again taken by the English in 1806,
and has since remained in their possession.

Vines were introduced and first planted
in the Cape of Good Hope on its being
colonized under Von Riebeeck in 1650;
but since the colony became a British possession, vines have increased more than
tenfold, and wine constitutes an important
article of commerce. The consumption of
the wine known as *Cape* was a few years
back very great, although by far the greater
part was doubtless used to sophisticate
sherry. This was frequently practised with
sherries for exportation, which claimed and
received a drawback of 5*s*. 9*d*. per gallon,
whilst probably only 2*s*. 11*d*. per gallon had
been paid as duty on two-thirds of the
quantity claimed upon. Cape wine enjoyed this advantage in respect to the
amount of duty for a great number of years.
In 1825, when the duty on French wines
was reduced to 7*s*. 3*d*. and all others to

4*s.* 10*d.*, the duty on Cape was 2*s.* 9*d.*, and in 1840, when 5 per cent. was added to all Customs' rates, Cape was charged 2*s.* 11*d.* Although in 1859 the consumption of Cape wine had reached its maximum, yet from the purposes to which it had been applied, and the publicity given to these frauds, the very name of Cape had become a by-word significant of want of quality. Such being the case, some ingenious speculator conceived the idea of discarding the old name Cape, and replacing it by the euphonious term, " South African;" and the perseverance of some enterprising firms succeeded for a time in making many believe in the discovery of a wine hitherto unknown. However on the 29th February, 1860, the edict went forth that Cape wine was to pay the same rate of duty as every other kind; and the consumption has consequently dwindled down to about one-tenth in the space of four years.

It will be seen by the following statement that the consumption and the per

centage which Cape bore to all other kinds
was :—

In 1831 consumption 539,584 galls. and 8·48 per cent.

| | | | | | | |
|---|---|---|---|---|---|---|
| 1841 | „ | 441,238 | „ | 7·10 | „ |
| 1851 | „ | 234,672 | „ | 3·74 | „ |
| 1859 | „ | 785,926 | „ | 10·84 | „ |
| 1860 | „ | 427,698 | „ | 5·81 | „ |
| 1861 | „ | 340,082 | „ | 3.16 | „ |
| 1862 | „ | 182,282 | „ | 1·86 | „ |

The wine known as *Constantia* is the
produce of the Cape of Good Hope, and
presents a marked contrast to the general
wine of the colony, differing not only in
quality but also in character. The reasons
assigned for this superiority are that the
soil of its growth is of a much lighter
nature, and the vines are of the Spanish
Muscatel species, whilst greater care is
taken in the manufacture of the wine, the
grapes being picked over and freed from
the stalks before they are pressed. The
vineyards are known as Great and Little
Constantia, growing both red and white
wine of a sweet character. The entire
quantity, in the most favourable years, does
not exceed one hundred pipes.

There is a common red wine, the produce of the Cape, known as *Pontac*. This
wine has been extensively used for mixing
with port, and in bad years has occasionally
been called on to serve in its stead. But
since the Cape wines have been put on the
same footing as other wines in respect to
duty, we seldom hear of them under their
proper names. As to Pontac, it might be
regarded as a thing of the past, since for
some considerable time there has been none
in the market. Do not, however, let us be
misunderstood. We by no means assert
that the wine itself has become extinct; for
Pontac is too useful for the purpose of
sophistication to be allowed to die out. It
finds its way to Bremen and Hamburg, and
forms an ingredient in the villainous compounds so largely concocted, and shipped
from thence principally for English stomachs. Our readers will find the subject
referred to more fully in a subsequent
chapter (page 205.)

Australia is the name adopted to desig-
nate all the countries which are considered

as forming the fifth great division of the globe. As it did not seem convenient to the geographers of the period to add these islands to Asia or to America, they wished to devise a name which should comprehend all of them, and at the same time express their position on the globe. The English adopted *Australasia*, the French *Oceanica*, and the Germans *Australia*, which latter name seems to have obtained the ascendancy.

The islands composing Australia . are situated partly to the south of Asia, and partly in the wide Pacific Ocean between Asia and America. From America they are divided by a wide and open sea, but there is no natural boundary which separates them from the islands belonging to Asia. The continent of Australia extends from east to west 2,400 miles, and from north to south about 1,700 miles, whilst its average breadth may be nearly 1,400 miles.

In 1830 the planting of vineyards commenced in Australia, several thousand cuttings of vines having been forwarded thence by Mr. Busby, who in the following year made a tour through the vineyards of France and Spain, in order to ascertain the best mode of cultivating and managing the vine, with a view to its propagation in the colonies of New South Wales.

Great expectations were formed of the capabilities of Australia as a wine-producing country, and from the favourable accounts received from time to time, much curiosity has existed as to the nature and qualities of the wines ; but although great industry appears to be shewn in the enterprise, we fear that Australia is not well adapted, either by soil or climate, for growing wine, and this opinion seems confirmed by the unsuccessful efforts of many years.

Some specimens of Australian wines were shewn at the International Exhibition of 1862, and the following is the Report of the Jurors concerning them :—

" The Australian colonies rank next in importance to the Cape in the cultivation of the vine, but owing to its comparatively recent introduction in these countries, the yield is yet very small, and quite insufficient for the home supply, the bulk of the wine used in the country being still imported from Europe. It is not likely, therefore, that for some years wine can be an article of much export. It is, however, interesting to watch the progress of the cultivation, and to observe the peculiar development of the vine. In this respect there is, as might be expected, in dealing with an area almost continental, and considering the numerous varieties of the vine that have been intro-duced from all parts of Europe, an infinite variety in the produce. We there find wines of the character of the German wines; others again more resembling the French wines ; whilst some have the substance and body of the wines of Spain. With care and time there is every prospect of these colonies becoming the great wine-growing countries of that part of the world."

# CHAPTER XX.

## A FEW PASSING REMARKS ON WINES.

" Trade, like blood, should circularly flow."

DRYDEN.

" Euclid was beaten in Boccaline for teaching his scholars a mathematical figure in his school, whereby he showed that all the lives both of princes and private men tended to one centre,—handsomely to get money out of other men's pockets and into their own."

SELDEN'S ' *Table Talk.*'

ABELAIS says, " Never did a great man hate good wine ;" and we are not prepared to controvert this dictum. Nevertheless it is somewhat to be wondered at that an intelligent nation should, in this enlightened age, consume so much *bad* wine. To what cause must this be attributed ? To the over credulity and want of discernment of John Bull, or to the clever tact of continental producers in the manufacture of their wines and expressly preparing them

for " the English market ? "   That a morbid
desire has been induced for low priced wines
cannot be denied; hence the introduction
of the once popular but short lived and
almost forgotten compound yclept " South
African," as well as the more recent delu-
sion and consequent disappointment experienced in regard to the lower class of
French wines.

We have, in a previous chapter, in treating of the wines of France, fully and freely
expressed our opinion on the commercial
treaty of 1862, and we have the satisfaction
of knowing that our views are those of
the trade generally.   That it has been
the means of bringing into the market an
amount of worthless trash unparalleled in the
history of the wine trade, no one will deny;
and such will ever be the case so long as
the alcoholic test is applied as the standard
of duty.   It is a partial return to the old
system of *ad valorem* duties long since
discarded.   If bad and worthless wine be
admitted at the 1*s*. duty, no one taking a
sensible or a sanatory view of the question

can tell us why wine that *can* be drunk
should pay 2*s.* 6*d.*, or in other words be
practically excluded, for such in fact must
be the effect of a differential duty. Of the
wine sold at the present day as Claret, very
little is entitled to that name, the bulk being
nothing more than the " vin ordinaire " or
common drink of France, and a considerable
quantity even worse. For Port, common
wines are substituted which are the produce
of either France or Spain, and known in
the trade under the terms of *French Reds*
and *Spanish Reds.* These wines are chiefly
shipped from Bremen or Hamburg; and
their price is from £8. to £14. per 115
gallons. Any one taking the trouble to
calculate this by the dozen will at once
perceive that the dishonourable tradesman
realizes a much larger proportion of profit
on the substituted sort, than the conscientious dealer who vends the veritable article,
and has to keep a large stock in order that
each vintage shall be properly matured.
In regard also to white wines, there is an
article known as *Hamburg Sherry*, ranging

from £8. to £12. per 108 gallons, which
most probably the outer world never heard
of, although they are unwittingly compelled
to swallow it.  If we ask why it is called
" Hamburg " Sherry, the answer will be,
because it is shipped from thence ; but
where is it *manufactured*,—we cannot say
*grown*, and what are the component parts
of this delectable *compound*,—this solace to
the robust and restorative to the invalid ?
Possibly a certain firm, whose grocer-agents
form the principal tributaries of supply can
inform us.  Since the foregoing remarks
were penned, our attention has been called
to a well written article, or rather series of
articles, in the 'Medical Times and Gazette,'
under the head of "Report on Cheap Wine,"
from which (November 26, 1864) we quote
the following :—" We will ask from what
unknown parts of the world these genuine
wines come, which form the staple of the
Hambro' chemists' laboratory.  When I
promised to report on cheap wine, it was
on the quality, price, and wholesomeness of
such as I could drink myself at my own

table. But I could not drink wine such as those which form the subject of this article, and therefore I cannot report on them fully. I could not venture to send my servant for these cheap wines, as I fear the honest fellow would give me warning directly. Now that Christmas and juvenile parties are coming upon us, let us hope that some friends of humanity will interfere to protect helpless women and children from cheap Hambro' port and sherry. I am certain that I have tasted at evening parties wine such as stands on the table before me as I write; and this is worth bearing in mind by the practitioner who is called in next day to treat a sick headache." The following is extracted from Ridley & Co.'s ' Monthly Circular,' January 7, 1864, under the head of " Hambro' Manipulations :"—" The harmony of trade in these cheap compounded liquids has for the last three months been frequently disturbed by Custom-house officials, who, as 'a matter of course, will not permit so-called " sherry" to pass into consumption without a careful analysis, to

ascertain whether it be veritable wine, or
mere sweetened spirits. At this date
several parcels are placed under stop, and
it appears likely, from the lengthened term
of detention, that they will be altogether
prohibited from being paid duty on as
wine. In our opinion such liquids have no
pretension to vinous attributes, being apparently compounded of spirit, *aqua pura*,
capillaire, and flavouring ethers, which, after
amalgamation, may perhaps be allowed to
feed on layers of raisins in the large vats
at Hambro.' The parcels now stopped
for investigation were shipped partly from
Bremen at £7. 15*s.*, and partly from Hambro' at £8. per 108 gallons free on board."
Her Majesty's Commissioners of Customs,
in their report for 1863, say,—" The *importation of spurious wines* into this country,
principally from *Hamburg*, is a subject that
has much engaged our attention during the
past year. The practice which of late years
has extensively prevailed of importing,
under the guise and denomination of wine,
an article containing a large per-centage of

spirit, but only a sufficient quantity, if any, of the known constituents of genuine wine to disguise the compound by the imitation of colour and flavour, is one which imposes a duty of great responsibility and difficulty on our officers, and is at the same time prejudicial to the interests both of the fair trader and the revenue." Mr. Shaw, referring to the same subject, says, "'South African' was a fortunate hit for 'Cape;' and we now see 'Elbe sherry' advertised as 'light and wholesome, suitable for either dinner or dessert, as stimulating as any wine imported, and peculiarly free from acidity.' Grapes do not thrive much on the Elbe, but potatoes grow in rich abundance in that favoured locality, and yield a fine native spirit; while the Elbe furnishes an ample supply of what in technical phrase is called 'liquor.' Both smell and taste give proofs of the scarcity of grape juice in this choice production; yet, really it does the Hamburgers great credit as chemists and manipulators, when we see what they contrive to send over to us, to tickle our palates with at such amazingly low prices. There is also 'Ebro port,' said to be from the north-east of Spain. Such designations prove what influence names are supposed to possess in this country." In Champagne again, thousands of dozens are imported, which, bottles and wine together, are not worth the duty. Mr. Kirwan, in an amusing book, entitled 'Host and Guest,' after expatiating largely on the delicacies of the table, briefly adverts to wines, and speaking of Champagne, says, "if gentlemen wish to obtain first-rate Champagne, they must go to a respectable wine merchant, and pay a fair price; they should avoid the cheap Champagnes with as much care as they would avoid the feculent water flowing out of Fleet Ditch into the Thames." This is undoubtedly correct, and applies to wines of all descriptions; for not only has the respectable wine merchant a reputation at stake, but his knowledge and experience are sufficient guarantee that he will select only such wines as are of good quality and likely to do him credit. Deception will always be practised more or less in every business; and the common light wines of France have offered a ready means of deceiving the public. Absurd professions are put forward, and fiction has supplied the place of facts with the most unblushing effrontery. Thus, we hear of parties represented as "having devoted a life's experience to the wine trade" who have never left the grocery counter, so that, in fact, the "experience" must have been acquired in dealing in *British* wines; and better would it be for the health and stomachs of Her Majesty's liege subjects if they obtained from the "Family Grocer" in the shape of cheap wines nothing more injurious than those homely beverages. Our facetious friend ' Punch ' makes a happy allusion to the practice of grocers being wine merchants, in an article headed ' In vino veritas.' *Little Girl.* "Please, sir, I want a bottle of shillin' port." *Grocer.* "My dear, we have nothing in ports as low as a shilling; but,— we've some delicious damson at 15*d.* and it's much the same thing." The following

is taken from Mr. Tovey's work on 'Wines
and Wine Countries.' "The opening of
the trade consequent upon the new tariff,
of which, however, we make no complaint,
has afforded an opportunity for the display
of some curious and amusing statements.
For instance—a Family Grocer 'informs
the public that he has received direct from
Bourdeaux several parcels of French wines,'
and he quotes:—

'Claret, Chateau Margaux . . . 32*s*. per dozen!
Claret, from the Chateau Giscours 50*s*. ,, ,, !!'

From this it would appear that the Giscours
is something very superior to Margaux.
But the "Family Grocer" still more asto-
nishes us. He quotes "Sherry direct from
Bourdeaux"

'Chateau d'Yquem . . . . 40*s*. per dozen!
Sherry, finest Sauterne . . . . 36*s*. ,, ,, !!'

We insert this literally, as taken from an
advertisement continually repeated in the
newspapers; and we do so in order to
show the absurdities committed by persons
who adopt a business, with the nature and
character of which they are wholly un-

acquainted; and which requires the most intimate knowledge of the various growths of wine, and an acquaintance with the countries from which they are procured. In all the higher professions there are diplomas, and licenses to practise from duly constituted authorities. There are degrees in divinity, in arts, in law, and in physic; and, descending to the humble trades, we find that all are apprenticed to their various callings. The mechanic of every trade will reject from the workshop any one who cannot by his indentures prove a right to follow his particular trade; and yet in a business which is scarcely second to any in importance, as regards the enormous revenue which it produces to the Government in the shape of duties, its benefit in the exchange of commodities with other countries, and the responsibility which it involves, in the diffusion of what is not only a luxury, but a necessary of life, there is no security to the public from the dishonest or ignorant adventurer."

In confirmation of this view we will quote

the opinion of one of the most practical and experienced men in the trade, Mr. Shaw, who says, " The wine trade is generally supposed to be easily understood, but no one who knows it will say thus much.  It is impossible for any one to be a good practical wine merchant in the shipping, the city-bottling, or the private trade, unless he knows every detail, not only at the docks and wharves, but in the cellar; and this latter part can only be learned by being able to do a cellarman's work."

Another eminent authority, Mr. Ruskin, speaking of the qualifications of a wine merchant, says, "he should understand to the very root the qualities of the thing he deals in, and the means of obtaining or producing it; and he has to apply all his sagacity and energy to the producing or obtaining it in a perfect state, and distributing it at the cheapest possible price where it is most needed."

Mr. G. R. Porter, of the Board of Trade, in his evidence before a select Committee of the House of Commons, in June, 1852, said : " The wine trade itself is much altered from the respectable character it used to bear; persons of inferior moral temperament have entered into it, and tricks are played, which in former times would not have been countenanced. The trade is getting a bad name."

We cannot conclude our chapter without referring to the following advice to persons about to purchase wines, and we commend it to the serious consideration of our readers. Mr. Cyrus Redding says, " Those who desire good and sound wines will seek the first growths, and to obtain them they must deal with merchants of established character, and give a remunerating price, otherwise they will be exposed to frauds on their purse and injury to their health." Mr. Tovey says, " If good wine is wanted, let them go to a respectable wine merchant, one of established reputation, who will be able to supply them, if he knows his business, with a pure wine at a less price, probably, than they would have to pay for a fictitious or adulterated article to the advertising man, who pays perhaps for puffing and advertising alone more than the whole year's profit of a merchant of established reputation, although the latter, probably, has more valuable stock in one bin than the puffing advertiser has in the whole of his cellar."

The following is the latest published return, giving the quantity of wine imported into the United Kingdom during the first seven months of the present year, as compared with that of the two previous years, and shews an increase of 1,703,419 gallons over 1863, and of 2,455,903 gallons over 1862. It will be observed that of this excess of 1,703,419 gallons, France furnishes but 324,051 gallons, whilst Spain contributes 1,474,747 gallons, or nearly five times the quantity of France.

" The quantity of wine imported into the United Kingdom in the first seven months of the present year amounted to 9,716,017 gallons. Compared with the imports in the same period of last year, an increase appears of 1,703,419 gallons, and with those in the seven months of 1862 of not less than

2,455,903 gallons. Towards the augmented supply of 1864, Spain has contributed as much as 1,474,747 gallons, France 324,051 gallons, Holland 30,546 gallons, Portugal 21,538 gallons, Italy 10,226 gallons, the Canary Islands 6,762 gallons, and Madeira 3,331 gallons. The British Possessions, Hamburg, and other countries, have, however, sent less by 36,949 gallons, 112,232 gallons, and 18,601 gallons respectively, as particularised in the subjoined tabular statement:—

| From | The first seven months of the years | | Increase. | Decrease. |
|---|---|---|---|---|
| | 1863. | 1864. | | |
| | Gallons. | Gallons. | Gallons. | Gallons. |
| British Possessions | 64,513 | 27,564 | — | 36,949 |
| Hamburg . . . | 257,432 | 145,200 | — | 112,232 |
| Holland . . . | 232,642 | 263,188 | 30,546 | — |
| France . . | 1,272,425 | 1,596,476 | 324,051 | — |
| Portugal . . | 1,940,241 | 1,961,779 | 21,538 | — |
| Madeira . . | 21,577 | 24,908 | 3,331 | — |
| Spain . . . | 3,773,671 | 5,248,418 | 1,474,747 | — |
| Canaries . . | 5,216 | 11,978 | 6,762 | — |
| Italy . . . . | 258,082 | 268,308 | 10,226 | — |
| Other Countries . | 186,799 | 168,198 | — | 18,601 |
| Totals . | 8,012,598 | 9,716,017 | 1,871,201 | 167,782 |
| | | | 167,782 | |
| Increase in 1864 . . . . . . | | | 1,703,419" | |

# CHAPTER XXI.

## ON THE CELLAR AND GENERAL MANAGE-MENT OF WINES.

" An English autumn, though it hath no vines,
    Blushing with Bacchant coronals along
The paths, o'er which the far festoon entwines
    The red grape in the sunny lands of song,
Hath yet a purchased choice of choicest wines;
    The claret light, and the Madeira strong.
If Britain mourn her bleakness, we can tell her,
The very best of vineyards is the cellar."
      BYRON, ' *Don Juan,*' *canto* xiii, *st.* 76.

THE chapter we are now entering upon refers to a subject interesting alike to the dealer and the connoisseur, since excellence of quality is as vitally important to the former, as it is ardently sought for and appreciated by the latter.

It is well known that wines, whether in cask or bottle, are liable, from natural as well as accidental causes, to certain mecha-

nical changes; and it is equally certain that
the choicest wine would be eschewed and
utterly condemned, if, when placed on the
table, it should be found to be out of condition. In taking a brief review of the
causes which may operate in producing
such a result, we must not overlook the
importance that should be attached to the
cellar itself. It frequently happens, especially in modern buildings, that little or no
consideration is given to the size or situation
of this most important adjunct; sometimes
the waste space under the staircase is
deemed sufficient for the purpose, irrespective of the constant tramping up and down
stairs, and consequent disturbance to the
wine. At other times the cellar is placed
next to the kitchen, or possibly some cup-
board in a recess on either side of a fire-
place is fixed on as the place for keeping (?)
the wine! Wine cellars are also to be
found in some back or front area, with a
temperature of zero in winter and 70° or
80° Fahr. in summer! Cellars and vaults
should be as remote as possible from streets

and other ways by which waggons pass, as
the vibration caused thereby is apt to dis-
turb the more delicate wines. Sir Edward
Barry, nearly a century back, writes,—
" The structure of a wine cellar ought to
be such as will most effectually defend the
wine from the frequent changes of the external air, adjacent fires, and the agitation
of carriages, and to preserve an equal
degree of heat, though some variations
must be unavoidable." Mr. Cyrus Redding
says, " A cellar should be a cellar in material, site, temperature, and solidity of construction." Lighter wines require a colder
cellar than strong wines ; but as a general
direction, the temperature of a cellar ought
always to be uniform, and should not be
under 40° nor above 55° Fahr. The size of
the cellar ought to be in proportion to the
quantity of wine for which it is designed.
The situation ought to be low and dry.
Double doors are an advantage, as one
may be closed before the other is opened,
and thus the changes of the external atmosphere cannot penetrate. Cellars in private

houses are rarely ventilated, and thus foul air is frequently generated. The back of a house is always preferable for a wine cellar, as the bottles are less likely to be shaken by the traffic of the street. The cellar of the practical wine merchant is so arranged as to have "a place for every-thing, and everything in its place;" and in like manner, a due regard to system and order should not be overlooked in the cellars of private individuals. The bins should be so arranged in regard to size as to be adapted to the quantity of wine each may be required to contain; thus, for Port or Sherry larger bins may be needed than for other descriptions of wine. The old practice of using saw-dust in binning wine is very objectionable, as when it becomes damp it generates heat, which is communi-cated to the wine.

Iron bins, as shewn in plate No, 1, are now very extensively used, not only by wine merchants, but also by private fami-lies, and they can be had according to the size of the cellar. As they are clean, take

up very little space, and are fitted so as to
receive shelves when wanted, there cannot
be a doubt of their superiority.   The following cuts will give an idea of their useful-
ness.    No. 2 represents a moveable bin
partly filled; and No. 3 shows another with
a guard and padlock, so that it may be
safely put in any open place.   The cost of
No. 2 is about 3s., and that of No. 3 about
6s. per dozen.   They may be had of the
manufacturers, Messrs. Farrow and Jackson,

For Arched Vaults.                    For Flat Ceilings.
Wrought-Iron Wine Bin.   No. 1.

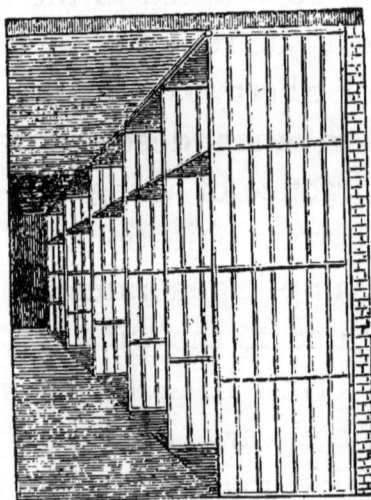

of Great Tower Street, who keep all articles
required for cellar use.

Registered Cellular Wine Bins; rest for each bottle. No. 2.

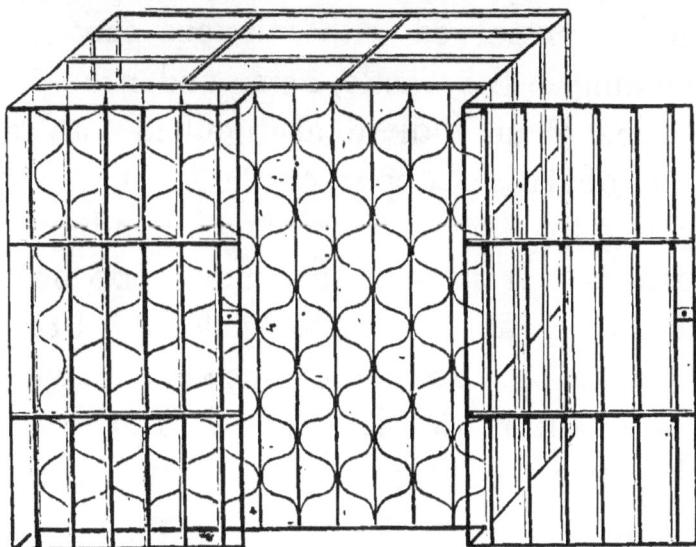

Moveable Iron Bin, with Lock. No. 3.

Wines ripen better and become more
matured in large casks than small ; thus if
the wine is to be kept in wood for any
length of time, butts or pipes are for this
reason to be preferred, and from them
quarter-casks and octaves can readily be
drawn to suit the views and meet the requirements of purchasers. It is to the
knowledge of wines and spirits maturing
better in bulk that led to the construction of
the great tun of Heidelberg. This monu-
ment of old times and good drinking (for
in days of yore it used to be filled with the
best Rhine wine) was constructed in 1591,
and is preserved with religious care in a
building in the Castle, being under the pro-
tection of an individual dignified with the
title of " the Cooper of the Castle," who
gains a livelihood by showing it to admiring
visitors. It is said to contain 600 hogsheads, or about 32,400 gallons. For a
more detailed account of this monster wine-
holder the reader is referred to ' Coryat's
Crudities,' vol. ii, p. 351. We apprehend,
however, that the vats or coolers of some

of our large Porter brewers of the present
day would be found of larger capacity.
We can testify to having seen, at the dis-
tillery of Messrs. Bishop and Sons, some
casks as large as 30,000 gallons, which are
employed in storing their British wines, in
which department that firm has long maintained a high repute.

The contents of a pipe of Port are 115 gallons; those of a butt of Sherry 108 gallons;
half of either of these is the hogshead,
which is double the quantity of the quarter
cask; this latter is again divided by the
octave, which contains about 13 gallons.

As while in the vaults or cellars the casks
are apt to become affected either by dry
rot or from damp, by which much fine wine
may be lost, it is desirable that the state of
the casks, as well as the condition of the
wine, should be occasionally looked to.
When any of the wine is drawn off, it is
necessary to fill up the void as speedily
as possible; or rack off the ullage into a
smaller cask, otherwise the air caused by
the vacuum renders it liable to become

sour. In some cases it is necessary to rack the wine from the *lees*, but this of course depends on the nature and condition of the wine, and is regulated according to the judgment of the dealer. When wines have been kept in wood for the period which experience has fixed as that proper for attaining maturity, whether they are intended for bottling or for draught purposes, they are fined down. Red wines are fined with white of eggs, and white wines with isinglass ; after which the cask must be left undisturbed for two or three weeks, at the expiration of which the condition of the wine should be carefully inspected, as a longer time might be required, or in some cases the operation might have to be repeated.

The process of bottling should take place in fine weather, if possible in March or October. The bottles must be perfectly clean and dry ; and if not new, care must be taken that no lead shots remain in them, as these render the wine deleterious. For Port wine, bottles that have been shotted are to be preferred, as from the natural affinity it has for the lead, the tartar of the wine is more readily deposited, and the wine becoming crusted arrives sooner at matured condition. The corks should be perfectly sound, and as elastic as possible, so that when driven home they may expand beyond the contracted part of the neck of the bottle, and thoroughly exclude the air. Among respectable wine merchants the recognized fair bottle is six to the gallon, but many others use a smaller size; consequently, when they sell at the same nominal price, they realize a greater profit. Bottles smaller than they should be are met with in all countries; but a neighbouring capital possesses an unenviable distinction in this respect. It is common to meet with bottles there containing only 60 to 65 *centilitres*, instead of 78 to 80, or running 370 bottles to the hogshead of Claret, instead of 270. Although exceedingly desirable to have some fixed standard of uniformity as to the contents of a bottle, it is a difficult question to grapple with, for not only would the

present bottled stocks present an obstacle,
but also while millions of old bottles exist
there seems no way of compelling the use
of any certain size. The term "quart"
bottle is entirely a misnomer, having origi-
nated with the small old gallon, now long
since discontinued.

But little advantage will attend the ac-
quisition of the best wine, if due care be
not taken to preserve and bring it to that
maturity and perfection which it can alone
derive from time,—a maxim, indeed, of
very ancient origin, for we read in the gos-
pel of St. Luke v., 39, " No man having
drunk old wine straightway desireth new ;
for he saith, The old is better." Wines
appear to be mellowed in two ways,—either
by the disengagement of a portion of their
aqueous particles and such ingredients as
obscure the delicacy of their flavour and
aroma, or by the more intimate union and
concentration of the remaining component
parts. No rule can be laid down for the
length of time wine should be kept, as it
would entirely depend—first, on the body

and strength of the wine, and, secondly, on the perfectness of the fermentation.

The subjoined sketch represents a useful invention, serving the double purpose of

Wooden Packing Cases, serving also as Bins.

packing wine for conveyance, and afterwards supplying the place of a bin or
cellaret by merely being placed upright.
These cases can be used in lieu of hampers,
and requiring no straw, cause no mess or
dirt in unpacking. They involve no risk of
breakage or pilferage in transit, and being
returned with empties can readily be refilled
with full bottles at pleasure. To the
bachelor, or those living in lodgings, their
utility and convenience must be evident, as
they can at any time be made secure by the
addition of an ordinary padlock to the lid.
They are made by Messrs. Spencer & Co.
of Fenchurch Street.

We have stated in a preceding chapter
that sparkling wines should always be laid
down (indeed, so much importance do we
attach to this matter, that at the risk of
being iterant we do not hesitate to repeat
the injunction); for if they are allowed to
remain upright, the corks, becoming dry,
shrink, and admit of the escape of the
carbonic acid gas, as well as the admission

of air, and the wine becomes vapid and valueless.

It may be thought that the process of cooling wines is of modern introduction, but that this practice was known to the Greeks and Romans is sufficiently evident. Indeed, the ancient wines were so congelated and solidified by inspissation, that in order to render them fluid they were subjected to heat, so that as a matter of necessity they had to be cooled. The vessels which contained the wine mixed with boiling water were immersed in snow, which had been preserved through the year in pits dug for that purpose, and such wine is particularly distinguished by Martial. This invention is ascribed by Pliny to Nero, who prided himself more on this improvement in luxury than Augustus did in encouraging the fine arts. Cicero, describing a supper of those days, alludes in particular to the symposium of Xenophon, where the wines were prepared by hot water and afterwards cooled in snow :—" Et pocula sicut in symposio Xenophontis minuta atque rorantia et refrigeratio æstate, et vicissim aut sol, aut ignis hiburnus."—' *De Senectute,*' *c.* 14.

The previous mode of cooling their wines, was by placing the *amphora,* or vessel in which the wine was contained, in a running stream. The following, written in the time of Augustus, will show such to have been the practice at that period :—

> " Quis puer ocius
> Restinguet ardentis Falerni
> Pocula pretereunte lympha ?"
> Horace.   O *de* ii, *book* 2.

Homer also refers to this primitive method of cooling wine :—

> " Such was the wine: to quench whose fervent steam,
> Scarce twenty measures from the living stream
> To cool one cup suffic'd : the goblet crown'd
> Breath'd aromatic fragrancies around."
> ' *Odyssey,*' *book* ix, 242.

We have referred in a previous chapter to the practice of icing wines, which is truly said to be destructive to every kind except Champagne and other effervescent wines ;

and even these kept long in ice are not to be compared to the same wine when brought out of a cold cellar. Few houses have cold cellars, and in such, cases in warm weather, cooling becomes necessary; but ten minutes or a quarter of an hour in the ice is quite sufficient to render it *frappé*, as our French neighbours call it. The practice of putting lumps of ice into the wine is a barbarous one; the individual must indeed be a Goth who would in this way spoil "Creaming Sillery" or "Pearl of the Rhine," and should be condemned to bad wine for the rest of his days, since it is evident that to him quality must be a matter of perfect indifference. We learn, from Dean Swift's journal of his visit to London in 1710, that this pernicious practice is not altogether of recent date. He says that Mr. Bertie, his medical man, would not let him put ice into his wine, remarking, " It is the very worst thing in the world, and gave my Lord Dorchester the bloody flux."

Within the last twenty years ice has been largely imported from Norway and other

parts, and has so conduced to our enjoyments as to have become one of our daily
requirements during a great part of the
year. The annual consumption of ice in
Paris is reckoned at 12,000,000 pounds
weight, exclusive of that used at the
Tuileries, the Palais Royal, and some of
the wealthier families, who are supplied
from their private ice houses. The city
charges an *octroi* duty on all the ice entering its walls, and finds a considerable item
of revenue in this tax. The usual mode of
cooling wine was to place the bottles in a
wine cooler filled with water, in which a
composition known as freezing powder was
dissolved. This preparation consisted generally of saltpetre, sal-ammoniac, and common
soda. The great consumption of ice, which
has now become an article of commercial
importance, has, however, superseded the
use of freezing mixtures, and we seldom
hear of their being employed at the present
day.

The operation of decanting wine is generally regarded as a very simple one ; but,

on the contrary, it is a matter of the utmost importance as regards the reputation of the wine; and presuming for the moment the article to be of superior quality, no conscientious host will think of deputing this duty to another. The best description of corkscrew is the lever; the bottle is placed on its end, and the cork extracted without the slightest agitation to the wine. The next care should be to see that the decanters are not only clean, but, what to the quality of the wine is still more important, dry; and unless this latter requisite is strictly attended to, the black bottle itself had better be used, for we feel assured that it is to this cause that much of the wine that is decanted is spoilt. Strainers are worse than useless, as they frequently impart a mouldy flavour. A steady hand and a watchful eye will prevent any deposit from entering the decanter.

We have now conducted our reader through the several intricacies of the cellar, discoursed with him on the various changes that wine is " heir to," and taken him into our confidence as to the different processes necessary to ensure its perfection, until we can in imagination picture the wine safely deposited on the sideboard in the very bloom of condition; we will, therefore, in closing this chapter, wish him health and appetite to enjoy it when placed on the table!

# CHAPTER XXII.

## History and Antiquity of Malt Liquors.

" Then studious she prepares the choicest flour,
The strength of wheat, and wines an ample store."
*' Odyssey,' book* ii—426.

HE art of brewing is of great antiquity, for although it may be impossible to fix a precise .date, yet it is nevertheless certain that the process of obtaining a fermented liquor from grain was known in the earliest ages. Herodotus, born 482 B.C., tells us that the Egyptians used a liquor made from barley. ('Euterpe,' ii—77.) From the oldest authorities we learn that the Egyptians had two sorts of beer, one called *zythus*, and the other *curmi*. Belon, in his 'Observations sur les Singularités trouvées en Grèce et en Asie,' inclines to the opinion that the *curmi* was made with

the whole grain, and that the *zythus* was,
like the *posca* of the Latins, a species of
*orgeat*, made with the flour of the grain,
kept in paste and diluted for the occasion.
Pliny, born A.D. 73, states, that in his time
beer was in general use amongst all the
nations who inhabited the western part of
Europe; and according to him, it was not
confined to those countries whose climate
did not permit the successful cultivation of
the grape. He mentions that the inhabitants of Egypt and Spain used a kind of
ale; and says that, though it was variously
named in different countries, it was univer-
sally the same liquor. ('Nat. Hist.,' *book*
xiv, c. 22.) Theophrastus and Diodorus
Siculus state that the Gauls called their
beer *zythus*: if this be true, it is not improbable that they received from the Egyptians both the name and the beverage.
Dion Cassius, born A.D. 155, alludes to a
similar drink amongst the people inha-
biting the shores of the Adriatic. ('De
Pannoniis,' *book* 49.) Tacitus, writing about
a century after the Christian era, states that

the ancient Germans " for their drink drew a liquor from barley or other grain, and fermented it so as to make it resemble wine." ('De Mor. Germ.,' c. 23.) Ale was also the favourite liquor of the Anglo-Saxons and Danes; it is constantly mentioned as one of the constituents of their feasts; and before the introduction of Christianity amongst the northern nations it was an article of belief amongst them that drinking copious draughts of ale formed one of the chief felicities of their heroes in the Hall of Odin. It is expressly named as one of the liquors provided for a royal banquet in the reign of Edward the Confessor. From the accounts given by Isidorus and Orosius, of the method of making ale amongst the ancient Britons and other Celtic nations, it is evident that it did not materially differ from our modern brewing. They state that "the grain is steeped in water and made to germinate; it is then dried and ground; after which it is infused in a certain quantity of water,

which is afterwards fermented." ('Henry's
Hist. England,' *vol.* ii, *page* 364.) Charle-
magne, in his capitulary *de villis*, directs
that among the workmen to be employed
on his farms, there shall be some who know
how to make beer. In Germany they were
at an early period famed for their beer and
ale. The towns of Lubeck and Rostock
stand foremost in the list for their double
beer, or *Brunswick mum*, as it was called;
at which places it was manufactured to an
enormous extent, the latter town exporting,
about the end of the sixteenth century, as
much as 800,000 barrels per annum. Beer
had been made an exciseable article in
this country by Parliament in the 19th of
Charles I, A.D. 1643, and it became a matter
of policy to tax the beer thus imported
from Germany. Excessive duties were consequently laid on these imports, amounting
at last, in the reign of Queen Anne, to the
enormous sum of fifteen shillings per barrel.
This heavy duty proved a prohibitory one,
and together with the improvements set
about by the brewers of this country at

that particular time, soon put a stop to the importation of beer.

In the Saxon Dialogues, preserved in the Cotton Library in the British Museum, a boy, who is questioned upon his habits and the uses of things, says, in answer to the enquiry what he drank,—"Ale, if I have it, or water if I have it not." He adds, that wine is the drink "of the elders and the wise." Of a favourite wassail or drinking song of the fifteenth century, the burden was,—

"Bring us home good ale."

"The good ale knights of England," as Camden calls the sturdy yeomen of that period, knew not, however, the ale to which hops in the next century gave both flavour and preservation; as although hops appear to have been employed in the breweries of the Netherlands in the beginning of the fourteenth century, they were not used in this country till nearly two hundred years afterwards. There were brewhouses in all the ancient monasteries; and to this day the

R

spot is frequently pointed out where the old brewhouse formerly stood.

There are some curiously quaint old ballads extant written in praise of ale. As a specimen we append one, contained in a work published in 1573, written by Dr. John Still, afterwards Bishop of Bath and Wells, called "A ryght pithy, pleasaunt, and merrie Comedie, intytuled ' Gammer Gurton's Nedle,' played not long ago in Christe's Colledge, in Cambridge." The ballad runs thus :—

> " Back and sides go bare, go bare,
>     Both foot and hand go colde;
> But belly God send thee good ale ynoughe,
>     Whether't be new or old."

In early periods of the history of England, ale and bread appear to have been considered as equally *victuals*, or actual necessaries of life. This appears from the various assizes or ordinances of bread and ale *(assisæ panis et cerevisiæ)* which were passed from time to time for the purpose of regulating the price and quality of these articles. In the 51st year of the reign of

Henry III. 1266), a statute was passed, the preamble of which alludes to earlier statutes on the same subject, by which a gra- duated scale was established for the price of ale throughout England. It declared that " when a quarter of wheat was sold for three shillings, or three shillings and four pence, and a quarter of barley for twenty pence, or twenty four pence, and a quarter of oats for fifteen pence, brewers in cities could afford to sell two gallons of ale for a penny, and out of cities three gallons for a penny; and when in a town *(in burgo)* three gallons are sold for a penny, out of a town they may and ought to sell four." In process of time this uniform scale of price became extremely inconvenient and oppressive; and by the statute 23 Henry VIII, c. 4, it was enacted that brewers should charge for their ale such prices as might appear convenient and sufficient in the discretion of the justices of the peace within whose jurisdiction they were situate. The price of ale was conse- quently regulated in this manner, and the quality was ascertained by officers of great antiquity called "*gustatores cervisiæ*,"—ale-tasters, or ale-conners.   These officers are still appointed in boroughs and towns corporate, and in many places, in compliance with charters or ancient custom, ale-conners are, to the present day, annually chosen and sworn, though the duties of the office have long since fallen into disuse.

# CHAPTER XXIII.

## On the Art of Brewing.

" Dost thou think, because thou art virtuous,
There shall be no more cakes and ale ?"
SHAKSPEARE. *' Twelfth Night,'* act ii, *sc.* 3.

REWING consists in the process of ex-
tracting a saccharine solution from
grain, and in converting that solution into
a fermented and sound spirituous beverage
called beer or ale. This art, although a
perfectly chemical one in nearly all its
stages, has not until comparatively lately
been indebted to chemistry for any of the
improvements which have been made in its
details. This we may attribute to the rare
occurrence in former days of a practical
chemist being engaged in the operation of
brewing. However, we find that within
the last few years, very great additions have
been made to our knowledge of this art,

particularly in our being acquainted with
that principle, by means of which the conversion of starch into sugar whilst in the
mash tun is brought about. Various other
improvements, affecting the mode and ap-
pliances, as well as the principles, of the
art of brewing, have also been adopted by
many of our leading firms, which contribute
largely to facilitate their means of production and supply.

The process usually followed by the
brewer may be divided into eight distinct
parts, independent of the malting : namely,
first, the grinding of the malt; secondly,
the operation of mashing; thirdly, the
boiling; fourthly, the cooling; fifthly, the fermentation; sixthly, the cleansing; seventhly,
the racking or vatting; and, eighthly, the
fining or clearing. In brewing the various
beers or ale, porter, and stout, three distinct sorts of malt are employed ;—the pale
or amber malt, the brown malt, and the
roasted or black malt. The first of these
alone is used for ales, indeed for the article
so extensively known as pale bitter ale very

light coloured malt only is applicable; the brown malt is the article in general use for giving the flavour to beer; and the roasted malt is chiefly used with the latter sort in imparting the requisite colour to porter and stout.

Many persons imagine that the peculiarity of the water in different districts produces the difference in the flavour of the beer brewed, but this is entirely erroneous; good beer may be brewed from hard or soft water, whether obtained from a well or a river. The most important point, as well as the most variable operation in the whole process of brewing, is the fermentation. Hardly any two counties follow exactly the same routine, some using very low heats, others very high; some cleansing early, others late; some skimming off the head, others continually beating it in; these, with a variety of other operations adopted at various stages of the process, give rise to the great variety of different flavoured beers which we have in this country. The proportion of hops to be used must depend so entirely on the beer in process of brewing, that no certain rate can be laid down ; but four pounds of new hops per quarter of malt should be ample for present use beers ; in beers for keeping, and again for exportation, as much as twenty-eight pounds per quarter have been used, but this would mainly depend on the time the beer is intended to be kept, and the nature of the climate to which it is consigned, as well as the duration of the sea voyage.

Of the different descriptions of malt liquors, porter is that of most general use, the London porter having attained a world-wide celebrity. Porter was first brewed in 1722. The malt liquor previously drunk consisted of three kinds—ale, beer, and " two-penny," and a mixture of two of either of these was a favourite beverage under the name of " half-and-half;" or a mixture was drunk called "three-threads," consisting of equal portions of each of the above kinds of liquor, for a draught of which the tapster had to go to three different casks. About 1722, Harwood, a London brewer, commenced brewing a malt liquor which was intended to unite the flavours of ale and beer, or ale, beer, and two-penny; and, having succeeded, he called his liquor " entire," or entire butt, a name intended to intimate that it was drawn from one butt only. Harwood's liquor obtained the name of " porter" from its chief consumption at that time by porters and labourers. The returns of the quantity of porter brewed by the several London brewers have not been published for the last few years, but it was stated at a treat recently given at the Crystal Palace, by Messrs. Truman, Hanbury & Co., to their *employés*, that the firm had sent out during the last twelve months over half a million barrels of porter.

# CHAPTER XXIV.

———

## SOME ACCOUNT OF BARLEY AND MALT.

" But the cheerful spring came kindly on,
　　And show'rs began to fall;
　John Barleycorn got up again,
　　And sore surpris'd them all."
　　　　　　　　　　　BURNS.

———

ALT is grain, usually barley, which has become sweet and more soluble in water, from the conversion of its starch into sugar by artificial germination to a certain extent, after which the process is stopped by the application of heat. The subject is an interesting one, but to do it full justice we should have to describe at length the details of the various manipulations to which the grain is subjected in the manufacture of malt; and as this would necessarily exceed the limits within which we have proposed to circumscribe ourselves, we cannot do better than refer the reader, who may wish to be fully acquainted with the details of malting, to the well-known work on 'Vegetable Chemistry,' by Dr. Thomson,* of Glasgow. By a recent enactment, agriculturalists have been permitted to use malt free of duty, for the purpose of feeding their stock. In 1860, the quantity of malt made in the United Kingdom is stated to be 5,347,999 quarters, of which 4,432,347 is given as being used by those engaged in the trade of brewing.

Barley (*hordeum distichon*) is too generally known to require a minute description. It is readily distinguished from other grain by its pointed extremities, and by the rough appearance of its outer skin, which is the corolla of the flower closely enveloping the seed, and, in most varieties, adhering strongly to it. Pliny ('Nat. Hist.' *book* xviii, *c.* 14), says that barley was one of the most ancient aliments of mankind. We read

---

* We regret to state that this amiable and scientific Professor died in August of the present year, at Richmond, in Surrey.

in Scripture (*Exodus* ix, 31) that it was cultivated in Egypt nearly 1500 years before Christ. Hippocrates mentions three different kinds of barley as being known in his time; these were probably H *distichon*, the common summer barley of England; H *vulgare*, spring barley; and H *hexastichon*, winter barley. In some climates two crops of barley may be reaped in the same year, one in spring from seed sown the preceding autumn, and one in autumn from a spring sowing. This explains a passage in *Exodus* (ix, 31), where the effect of the hail is mentioned which desolated Egypt, in consequence of the refusal of Pharoah to let the children of Israel depart : " The flax and the barley were smitten, for the barley was in the ear, and the flax was bolled ; but the wheat and the rye were not smitten, for they were not grown up." Commentators agree that this event happened in the month of March ; the first crop of barley was, therefore, nearly ripe, and the flax ready to pull ; but the wheat and the rye sown in the spring were not yet sufficiently advanced in growth to be injured by the hail.

Thus barley, according to the ancient authors, formed a principal part of the food of man in the early ages; and continues so to this day in many countries where the progress of agriculture and the increase of wealth have not yet enabled the inhabitants to exchange the coarser barley loaves for the more palatable and nutritious wheaten bread. In seasons of dearth, the Paris brewers have been forbidden to make beer, so that the grain should be exclusively applied to the purpose of food. *Ordonnances* of the Prévôt de Paris appeared to this effect in 1415, and again in 1482. An *arrêt* of the council renewed this interdiction in 1693, and two others to a like effect appeared in 1709 and 1740. According to Einhof, 100 parts of ripe barley corns consist of husk 18·75, meal 70·05, and water 11·20.

## CHAPTER XXV.

### Some Account of Hops.

" The hop for his profit I thus do exalt,
* It strengtheneth drink, aud it flavoureth malt;
And being well brew'd long kept it will last,
And drawing abide, if ye draw not too fast."
Tusser. *' Five Hundred Points of Good
Husbandry.* 1557.

HE hop (*humulus lupulus*) is a perennial rooted plant with an annual twining stem, which, on poles or in hedges, will reach the height of from twelve to fifteen feet or even more. It is a native of Britain and most parts of Europe, and is chiefly found in hedges, flowering in June, and ripening its seeds in September. The generic name of the plant, *humulus*, is derived from *humus*, fresh earth,—the hop growing only in rich soils; and the specific name of the common hop (lupulus) is a contraction from *lupus salictarius*, the name

by which it was, according to Pliny, formerly called, from the fact of its growing
among the willows, to which, by twining
round and choking up, it proved as destructive as the wolf to a flock.  It is rather
curious that an allusion to the wolf is also
contained in the ancient British name of
the plant, *llewig y blaidd*, or bane of the
wolf.  The current name, *hop*, seems to
proceed from the Anglo-Saxon, *hoppan*, to
climb.  The proverbial distich given in
' Baker's Chronicle '—

> " Turkey, carps, hoppes, piccarel, and beer,
>   Came into England all in one year,"

has led to the impression that hops were
not known in this country till the reign of
Henry VIII, or about the year 1524; but
the plant was known long previously, for it
grew wild by the sides of hedges and upon
banks more or less throughout England,
and its young shoots were and still are
often gathered by the villagers, and boiled
as an esculent vegetable.  The young
shoots of the cultivated hop are sometimes
gathered in the spring, and eaten as aspa-

ragus, being sold under the name of hop-
tops.

It appears that the *culture* of the plant
was not adopted in this country until the
time of Henry VIII, and that our knowledge on the subject was derived from
Flanders. Before that period hops had
been imported and used on a limited scale
in the preparation of beer. In the reign
of Henry VI. (A.D. 1428), the hop was
petitioned against as "a wicked weed."
Hops are first mentioned in the English
Statute Book in 1552, in the Act 5 Edward
VI, chap. 5, where lands "set with saffron
or hops" are mentioned among other ex-
ceptions to the operation of the statute
itself, which enacted that so much land
should be kept in tillage as had been
at any time in tillage since the first of
Henry VIII. It does not appear, however,
that the culture of hops proceeded very
rapidly at first, for so late as the reign of
Queen Elizabeth they were fetched in considerable quantities from the Low Countries ; but from an Act of Parliament in the

year 1603, it seems that hops were at that time grown in great abundance. In the reign of James I, however, we find that the produce was not equal to the increased consumption, as there is a statute (1608) against the importation of damaged or inferior foreign hops.

There is only one species of the hop plant under cultivation, but it has several varieties, such as the red-bind, the green-bind, the white-bind, and some others; but hops are distinguished by the growers under different names, such as the Flemish, Canterbury, Golding's, Farnham, Jones', and some other similar titles. The most productive grounds are those which have a deep rich loamy surface, with a sub-soil of deep brick earth; and this kind of land forms the principal part of the hop gardens in the eastern division of Kent, which is proverbially the great hop growing county of England. For a lengthened description of the mode of cultivating the hop, and of the general management of a hop plantation, we cannot do better than refer the reader to

Mr. Loudon's 'Encyclopædia of Agriculture.'
The expense of forming a new hop ground
is exceedingly heavy, being estimated in
many districts at from £70. to £100. per
acre. The duration of a hop plantation on
a good soil varies from fifteen to thirty
years ; but in general they begin to decline
after the tenth year. The plant is liable
to so many diseases, and is exposed to so
many casualties, that the produce is subject
to very great fluctuation. There are too
many modifying influences of soil, climate,
season, and other adventitious circumstances, for any established rules to be laid
down for general adoption in hop culture;
but the more we can trace effects to their
causes, and ascertain the mode in which
nature operates, the nearer we are to fixed
principles and a sure rule of practice. In
some seasons the growth of an acre amounts
to twenty hundred-weight, whilst in others
it does not exceed two or three hundred-
weight, or even less. In middling soils
from nine to ten hundred weight are considered a fair average crop, and from twelve

to fourteen as a good one. Indeed, in bad seasons, it has not unfrequently happened that whole fields have remained unpicked, from the produce not being sufficient to remunerate the cost of labour and the amount of duty. In 1860 there were 46,271 acres of hops in cultivation in the United Kingdom, on which a duty of £53,489. was paid. The duty on hops having since been abolished, no later return has been published. For some few years hop grounds had been gradually diminishing, owing no doubt to the precarious nature of the crop. The repeal of the duty, however, has caused a re-action, and much new planting is going on. Only suitable soils are selected, and the best sorts of hop root set; and in a few years hop gardens will be greatly extended, and English hops in greater competition with foreign importations.

# CHAPTER XXVI.

## Opinions on Malt Liquors, medical and otherwise.

"Be careful not to provoke the Giver by abusing the gift."—Taylor.

Beer differs from wine in several important particulars. Thus it contains a much larger quantity of nutritive matter, and a considerably less proportion of alcohol. That its inebriating property does not wholly depend on the alcohol which it contains, is shown by comparing the quantity of spirit obtained by Mr. Brande, from brandy, wine, and porter. From his experiments, it appears that the same amount of spirit is contained in the following quantities of wine, brandy, and beer :—

Port wine . . . . 1·00
Claret . . . . . 1·52
Champagne . . . 1·82
Brandy . . . . . 0·43
Burton ale . . . . 2·58
London porter . . . 5·46
Small beer . . . . 18·16

Now, if the intoxicating quality of beer depended on the spirit alone, the effect of five and a half pints of London porter, or two and a half pints of Burton ale, should be equal only to that of a pint of port wine; whereas, its actual inebriating power greatly exceeds this.

That beer is nutritive, and, when used in moderation, salubrious, can scarcely be doubted. It proves a refreshing drink, and an agreeable and valuable stimulus and support to those who have to undergo much bodily fatigue. The poor labourer who has repeatedly experienced its invigorating property, will by no means admit the truth of Franklin's assertion,* that a penny

* ‘ *Select Works*,’ by W. T. Franklin, *vol.* i, *p.* 36. 1818

loaf and a pint of water yield more nourishment than a pint of beer.

Various medical writers have placed a high value on the properties possessed by the hop. Dr. Paris tells us that the most useful quality in beer comes from the hop. " Independently," says he, " of the flavour and tonic virtues which hops communicate, they precipitate by means of their astringent properties the vegetable mucilage, and thus remove from the beer the active principle of fermentation; without hops, therefore, we must either drink our malt liquors new and ropy, or old and sour." Dr. Pereira says " the hop operates as a tonic and assists digestion." Dr. Chapman, in his 'Therapeutics,' recommends the use of the hop in nephritis, and Dr. Maton speaks highly of its utility in arthritic rheumatism, and asserts that it allays pain, produces sleep, and modifies the frequency of the pulse, at the same time that it increases its firmness. Dr. Desroches also published a 'Dissertation on the Hop,' in 1803. Dr. Ives, speaking of *lupulin*, the active principle of the hop, says, " It frequently induces sleep, and quiets nervous irritation, without causing costiveness, or impairing, like opium, the tone of the stomach, and merely increasing the primary disease." A pillow of hops is occasionally employed in mania, and those cases of neuralgic pains in which inquietude and restlessness prevail; and in hop countries it is a popular remedy for want of sleep. The benefit said to have been obtained from it by George III., for whom it was prescribed by Dr. Willis in 1787, brought it at that time into considerable use. As regards the tonic and restorative properties of ale and stout to the invalid, we have the testimony of medical men in all ages; and the many published opinions of our leading physicians in favour of " bitter ale," evidence the fact of it being " recommended by the faculty."

It would be absurd to advert to beer otherwise than as a national beverage, since it has become one of the necessaries of life amongst all classes, if we except, perhaps, the "upper ten thousand," who sip their *château* or their *cabinet* wines. But let us for a moment take the case of the industrious artizan, the toil-worn labourer, or the humble wayfarer. To him beer is an article of daily sustenance, and is, in his limited dietary table, an item of as much importance as any comprised under the head of food. And yet there are individuals, who, arrogating to themselves the functions of sole judges in such matters, seek to enforce a *total prohibition* of these articles; and failing in such object, they fall back upon the *permissive use* of them under certain regulations. This project has failed also, and we venture to say that it will be many years before a similar measure is brought before an English Parliament. It cannot be asserted that drunkenness has increased, for statistics shew that it has diminished surprisingly during the last fifty years. Doubtless, the force of example has had its influence in this respect, for during that time the customs of the higher classes have undergone a material change in regard to excessive drinking, and the habits of the people have consequently improved in like proportion. It is not, however, by penal enactments that a nation can be coerced into habits of sobriety ;—take Scotland, for instance, where, notwithstanding the stringent laws on the subject, drunkenness prevails to a fearful extent. If we seek to impress on the minds of the lower orders a necessity for improving their moral and social position, we must enlighten the working man on such subjects as he may be ignorant of, and afford to his children the means of education. And no class do we find, as a body, more zealous in this good work than those engaged in the brewing interest. We will instance the Whitbreads, Buxtons, Hanburys, and a long list of philanthropists, whose names have been associated with the great cause of humanity and civilization. We could also mention others connected with our leading breweries, who have not only contributed most munificently to the vast charities of the metropolis, but have taken a leading part in the subject of education, as well as in all matters tending to ameliorate the condition of the lower classes. We would say to our Someses and our Lawsons, if you would accomplish the object you profess to have in view, " Go thou and do likewise !"

The exportation of malt liquors has of late years, as a matter of commerce, grown into a trade of great importance. A correspondent at Melbourne writes, " Although the shipment of beers in bulk will most likely keep up to its present quantity, yet a vast increase in the export of bottled stock has taken place, and the demand is increasing to a great extent, owing to certain consignees having been in the habit of emptying the casks on their arrival, and sending them up the country re-filled with an inferior article under colour of the original brand." The following statement of exports is taken from the last return. " The exports of beer and ale during the six months of this year ending June 30th, shew a slight increase; having amounted to 261,598 barrels, against 259,386 barrels in the corresponding period of 1863, and

248,137 barrels in the like period of 1862. There has been a decrease in the quantity of beer and ale shipped to Australia this year; the exports in that direction having been only 68,439 barrels, against 93,547 barrels in the corresponding period of 1863. The United States, however, took 7,608 barrels this year, against 3,398 barrels in 1863; the West Indies 13,247 barrels this year, against 11,327 barrels in 1863; India 90,374 barrels this year, against 83,744 barrels in 1863; and other countries 81,930 barrels, against 67,370 barrels in 1863. The value of the beer and ale exported during the first six months of the present year was £940,247. against £886,918. in 1863, and £814,229. in 1862."

# CHAPTER XXVII.

## On Distillation and Rectification.

> " There's a spirit above, and a spirit below,
> A spirit of joy and a spirit of woe;
> The spirit above is the spirit divine,
> The spirit below is the spirit of wine."
> *On the vaults of a chapel being used as wine-cellars.*

E have no historical record of the period when the distillation of spirits was first known. The Greeks and the Romans were ignorant of ardent spirits; and from the absence of any evidence to the contrary, we must assume that the art of distilling was not known until long afterwards.

The use of the still appears to have been well known in the time of Geber, who lived in the seventh century, and who describes very accurately the process of distillation by the alembics *per descensorium et filtrum,* in his work, entitled ' Liber Investigationis Magisterii.' It has been stated that Albucasis, who is supposed to have lived in the twelfth century, taught the method of procuring spirit from wine; but as the process of distillation was evidently known long before his time,* it is equally certain that his predecessors had submitted fermented liquors to this operation. Arnauld de Villeneuve, a physician of the thirteenth century, is the first author who speaks explicitly of an intoxicating spirit obtained by the distillation of wine, and he considers it to be the universal *panacea* so long sought after in vain. His disciple, Raymond Lully, was acquainted with spirit of wine (which he called *aqua ardens*), as well as of the mode of depriving it of water by means of some alkali. Morewood considers the Chinese to have been acquainted with this process long before the rest of Asia, Africa, and Europe. In his ' Essay on Inebriating

---

* Dr. Royle's 'Essay on the Antiquity of Hindoo Medicine,' p. 46.

Liquors,' page 107, he says, " In China, a country which has preserved its civil polity for so many thousand years, the art of distillation was known far beyond the date of any of its authentic records. The period of its introduction into that country, in common with the rise and progress of other chemical arts, is, however, concealed amidst the darkness of ages. But taking dates as we find them, sanctioned by respectable authority, and leaving the assumed antiquity of the nation as a point for the discussion of chronologists, we are certainly led to attribute to the people of this empire the merit of an invention which seems to have eluded the grasp of the human intellect in the rest of Asia, Africa, and Europe, until a more advanced period in the history of the world."

The preparation of alcohol may be divided into three stages :—the production of a fermented vinous liquor; the preparation from this of an ardent spirit by distillation ; and, lastly, rectification or purification.

When vegetable substances are placed in

contact with air and moisture, they undergo that kind of decomposition which is denominated *fermentation*. The products of this process vary at different periods or stages; and on this depends the distinction into kinds or varieties of fermentation. Thus, starchy liquids, under some circumstances, become saccharine; the process being termed the *saccharine* fermentation. Sugar dissolved in water, and mixed with nitrogenous matter, is converted into carbonic acid and alcohol; and to this process the name of *vinous* fermentation is applied. Under some circumstances, mannite, lactic acid, and a syrupy mucilage, are formed by the action of the nitrogenous or albuminous principles of vegetable juices on the sugar; this change has been denominated the *viscous* or *mucilaginous* fermentation. Vinous liquids are capable of generating acetic acid, and the process is called *acetous* fermentation. Lastly, most vegetable substances are slowly converted into gases, and a substance called vegetable mould, constituting the process termed the *putrefactive* fermentation.

The liquid obtained by the vinous fermentation has received different names according to the substance from which it is obtained. When procured from the fresh juices of fruits, as grapes, currants, gooseberries, &c., it is denominated *Wine;* from a decoction of malt and hops, *Ale,* or *Beer;* from the expressed juice of apples, *Cyder;* that of pears, *Perry;* and from a mixture of honey and water, *Mead.* Fermented infusions of barley (raw grain and malt), prepared by distillers for the production of ardent spirit, are technically termed *Washes.*

By the distillation of a vinous liquid we obtain ardent spirit. When grape wine is employed, the spirit is called *Brandy;* when the vinous liquid is obtained by the fermentation of molasses or treacle, the spirit is termed *Rum;* when the vinous liquid is a fermented infusion of rice, the spirit is named *Arrack,* and is principally used at the present day to impart an agreeable flavour to punch. When the liquid is a fermented infusion of grain, commonly termed wash, the spirit is denominated

*Corn Spirit;* the various liquors called *Gin,*
*Hollands,* and *Whiskey,* are corn spirits
flavoured.

The object of the rectifier is to deprive
ardent spirit of its volatile oil and water.
This is effected by repeated distillations,
and by the use of certain alkalies, which,
by their powerful affinity for water, check
the rise of this fluid in distillation. In this
way is procured the liquid chemically known
as *Rectified Spirit,* more commonly called
*Spirit of Wine,* which is sent out by the
rectifiers as high as 56 *per cent. over proof,*
and is used by hatters, varnish-makers, &c.,
for readily dissolving the various gums
used in their respective businesses.

*Alcohol* is a limpid, colourless, inflam-
mable liquid, having a peculiar and pene-
trating odour, and a burning taste. Its
specific gravity at 60° F., is 0,7947; at 68° F.,
it is 0,792—0,791. No means of solidifying
it are at present known. It boils at 172° F.;
every volume of the boiling liquid gives
488,3 volumes of vapour, calculated at
212° F. It is very combustible, and has a

strong affinity for water. In atmospheric air it burns with a pale blue flame, giving out a very intense heat, and generating carbonic acid and water; but depositing no soot, unless the supply of oxygen be deficient. The colour of the flame may be variously tinted,—as, yellow by chloride of sodium, whitish violet by chloride of potassium, green by boracic acid or any salt of copper, carmine by chloride of lithium, crimson by chloride of strontium, and greenish yellow by chloride of barium. The component parts of alcohol are, according to Lavoisier, 28·53 carbon, 7·87 hydrogen, and 63·4 water.

# CHAPTER XXVIII.

---

## ON BRITISH AND FOREIGN SPIRITS.

" Gie him strong drink until he wink,
 That's sinking in despair;
An liquor guid to fire his bluid,
 That's prest wi' grief and care;
There let him bouse an' deep carouse
 Wi' bumpers flowing o'er,
Till he forgets his loves or debts,
 An' minds his griefs no more."
   BURNS. *Proverbs* xxxi, 6-7 *versified.*

---

HE British spirit so extensively used and known as Gin is obtained by distillation from fermented infusions of barley, and its quality is mainly determined by the cleanness of the spirit; for if drawn over too closely it becomes tainted by the *feints*, or last washings, and has to be subjected to re-distillation. Too much importance, therefore, cannot be attached by dealers to the quality of the spirit itself, as well as to the flavouring employed, so that no one flavour shall unduly preponderate. It is not permitted stronger than 17 *per cent. under proof,* which is the strength generally sent out to the trade, but small dealers, whose consumption is more limited, are frequently supplied at 22 *per cent. under proof.* It was first introduced to the public in imitation of the Dutch spirit, Hollands, which was formerly in much more extensive use than at the present day.

Hollands is imported chiefly from Rotterdam, and is obtained in a similar manner to gin, except that we are told buck-wheat is frequently used in its manufacture. It is of much fuller flavour, caused principally by the juniper berries employed in the flavouring being used in their green or unripe state. It was formerly in great demand in this country, but within the last fifty years gin has very materially superseded the consumption of hollands. The best qualities are distinguished by particular marks or brands.

Whiskey is the Irish word *uisque,* water. The name which the Irish give to this dis-

tilled spirit is *uisque beatha*, or water of life.
Usquebaugh, the name of a cordial at one
time in request, is the same two words in
a compound form. Whiskey is manufactured both in Ireland and Scotland, and in
each country is very extensively used. Each
possesses a flavour peculiar to itself, and
those who have attached themselves to
whiskey of any particular district, are frequently unwilling to take up with any other,
however fine may be the quality. Indeed,
more prejudice exists in regard to whiskey
than any other spirit. Thus, the Scotch-
man will be found to affirm that the Irish
drawn whiskey is the most smoky, whilst
our Hibernian friend as stoutly maintains
the contrary. But, nationality apart, very
fine specimens of whiskey are to be met
with in both countries, the great desidera-
tum being that the dealer should, in his
selection, make choice of such samples as
are distinguished by the purity of the spirit
and the fineness of the *bouquet* or aroma.
This done, let the article be well matured,
for no spirit more improves by age than

whiskey; and this is a point dealers too often disregard.

Rum is supposed to derive its name from the terminal syllable of the word *saccharum*, sugar being the article of which it is the product. It is a spirit distilled from the sugar cane, that is, either from cane juice, the scummings of the juice from the boiling house, molasses, or from *dunder*, which is a term given to the lees of former distillations, so called from the Spanish word *redundar*, to overflow. As the entire juice of the cane is not necessary for making rum, the distillation is carried on in conjunction with the manufacture of sugar. It has been calculated that a plantation yielding on an average 200 hogsheads of sugar and 130 puncheons of rum annually, must consist of about 900 acres. The best rum is made from the uncrystallized syrup called treacle or molasses. The rum consumed in the United Kingdom is almost entirely the produce of the West Indies, that of the island of Jamaica being distinguished by its superior quality. It is the liquor which has always been used throughout the Navy, the Government contracts for the supply of which average for the last three years the enormous quantity of 243,580 gallons annually, and in time of war the consumption is more than doubled. The demand for rum has, however been gradually declining in England for many years, and is quite insignificant in Scotland and Ireland.

Brandy is the alcoholic or spirituous portion of wine, separated from the aqueous part, colouring matter, &c., by the process of distillation. The word is of German origin, *brantwein*, meaning burnt wine, or wine which has undergone the operation of fire. Brandy is prepared in most countries, as France, Spain, Portugal, &c., that obtained from France being by far the most esteemed. It is procured not only by distilling the wine itself, but also by fermenting and subjecting to distillation the *marc*, or residue of the last pressings of the grape; but this latter has a more acrid flavour, and is much inferior in quality. For the production of brandy it is more advantageous to distil wines which are on the decline than those which are perfect in flavour; not only because they are cheaper, but because the spirit is in a more developed state in them. Various kinds of stills and alembics are employed; probably no two manufacturers use the same description of apparatus. Although brandy is imported into England from various places in France, as from Bourdeaux, Rochelle, and Nantes, yet that of Cognac, a town in the department of Charente, is preferred to all of them; and M. Aubergier assigns as a reason for this superiority, because it is obtained from white wine, fermented so as not to become impregnated with the oil of the grape skin. Brandy began to be distilled in France about the year 1343, but it was prepared only as a medicine, and was considered as possessing such marvellous strengthening powers, that the physicians termed it *Eau de vie,* the water of life, a name it still retains. Raymond Lully, in the thirteenth century, considered this admirable essence of wine to be an emanation from the Divinity, and that it was intended to restore and prolong the life of man. Of the Brandy exported from France this year, England takes 84,439 hectolitres, against 54,166 in 1863, and 34,000 in 1862.

Thick syrupy spirits, variously flavoured, are called *compounds;* those imported from abroad are termed *liqueurs.*

Before the true means of determining the quantity of alcohol in spirits were known, the dealers were in the habit of employing a very rude method of forming a notion of the strength. A given quantity of spirits was poured upon a portion of gunpowder in a dish, and set on fire. If at the end of combustion the gunpowder continued dry enough, it took fire and exploded; but if it had been wetted by the water in the spirit, the flame of the alcohol went out without setting the powder on fire. This was called *the proof.* Spirits which kindled gunpowder were said to be above proof; those that did not set fire to it were said to be below proof. From this origin of the term " proof," it is obvious that its meaning must have been very indefinite.

From an official return, just published, it appears that in the first eight months of the present year, ending the 31st of August last, the declared value of British spirits exported was £396,796.

# CHAPTER XXIX.

## CONCLUSION.

" Go, little booke, to suttle world,
　　And shew thy simple face,
And forward passe, and do not turne,
　　Nor slacken in thy pace :
Desire those men that like thee not,
　　To lay thee downe againe,
Till some sweete nappe and harmless sleepe,
　　Hath settled troubled brayne."
RIMBAULT's ' *Collection of Ancient Ballads and MSS.*'

OUR task is now approaching towards a close, and in the interchange of those little amenities which fellow-travellers may be expected to indulge in on parting company, we trust that our kind readers have not journeyed through these pages without some little interest being excited or awakened on the subject of Wines. We cannot boast of the amount of self-denial claimed by a cotemporary writer,* who states that " he neither writes for fame

---

\* Mr. Tovey.

nor profit;" for we confess that we are not wholly insensible to the one, nor utterly regardless of the other. But, at the same time, we must be understood as entering on our labours *con amore*, actuated by an earnest desire to be useful in our generation so far as our poor ability serves. Without laying claim to that contentedness for small blessings so pithily expressed by a noble bard,

" And though these lines should only line portmanteaus,
   Trade will be all the better for these cantoes,"\*

we shall be perfectly content, if, from our brief and imperfect description, some few may so far benefit as to be enabled to distinguish between a genuine article and one that is worthless. The value of *good* wine need not be insisted on. To the invalid, the weakly, the infirm, the *bon-vivant*, the occasional wine-drinker, as well as even to those who but seldom indulge in the luxury, the question of *quality* is one of very great importance. Wine may be truly said to be

---

\* Lord Byron's '*Don Juan,*' *canto* xiv. *st.* 14.

"nil nisi bonum." And, in order that the
public may obtain *good* wines, it is necessary
that they should be so far familiarized
with the subject as to be able to discrimi-
nate for themselves. Light is to the mind
what food is to the body; and if our remarks, imperfectly expressed, but offered
in all sincerity, should be found to have
thrown any additional light on this important subject, our time will not have been
unprofitably occupied.

Had it formed any part of our plan in
this brief summary, without entering deeply
into the question in a social or political
point of view, much might be adduced as
to the cheering influence and beneficial
effects of vinous liquors upon the mind and
body, when obtained in a state of purity,
and used with moderation. It is true that
certain writers[*] have indulged in puerile

---

[*] "Dr. Close, Dean of Carlisle, recommends the mixing
of wine with assafœtida, with the object of disgusting
people with this beverage." '*West End News*,' October 29,
1864. With due submission, we would ask the reverend
divine how he construes the passage, 1 Timothy v. 23;
wine is there recommended without the adjunct.

arguments, and have adopted theories as illogical as inconclusive; but we have yet to learn that occasional excesses justify a total deprivation. However, it is not our province at present to challenge opinions or to invite argument, our little work being framed rather with a view to amusement and information. Doubtless these things, in common with all other blessings, were sent for our enjoyment; and in the exercise of that enjoyment, we can, by limiting our desires within the bounds of moderation, best show our appreciation of the many advantages we possess. Good wine or good ale cannot be said to be exceptional articles among "the good things of this life;" but we should so use them, that "digestion may wait on appetite, and health on both." It is the *use* and not the *abuse* we should advocate. "Medio tutissimus ibis."

Few writers know more of the habits and temperament of mankind, and few men can form a better estimate of the social condition of the working classes and of their wants and requirements, than our popular and talented author, Charles Dickens. We will quote his views on the subject ('All the Year Round,' *April* 18, 1863) :—" The cause of temperance is not promoted by any intemperate measures. It is intemperate conduct to assert that fermented liquors ought not to be drunk at all, because, when taken in excess, they do harm. Wine, and beer, and spirits, have their place in the world. We should try to convince the working man that he is acting foolishly if he gives more importance to drink than it ought to have. But we have no right to inveigh against drink, though we have a distinct right to inveigh against drunkenness. There is no intrinsic harm in beer; far from it; and so, by raving against it we take up a line of argument from which we may be broken quite easily by any person who has the simplest power of reasoning. The real temperance cause is injured by intemperate advocacy; and an argument that we cannot honestly sustain is injurious to the cause it is enlisted to support."

The opinions of other eminent authorities can be quoted to the like effect, and the highest medical testimony might be adduced to confirm these views. Want of space, however, prevents our enlarging on the subject, and reluctantly compels us to bring our remarks (considerably extended beyond our original intention) to a close; and we cannot do so in more appropriate terms than in respectfully bidding our kind readers farewell, and wishing

## A Happy New Year to All!

LONDON: J. DAVY AND SONS, PRINTERS,
137, LONG ACRE.

# INDEX.

—◆—

## WINES, &c.

| | PAGE |
|---|---|
| Angelico | 194 |
| Aidanil | 185 |
| Albano | 166 |
| Alisa | 194 |
| Aloupka | 185 |
| Amontillado | 92 |
| Amphora, The | 4, 5, 6 |
| Anacreon | 44 |
| Aristotle | 45 |
| Assmanhausen | 147 |
| Athenæum, The | 103 |
| Baccius, Andrea | 4, 49 |
| Bacon, Lord | 48 |
| Baillie, Mrs. | 122, 123 |
| Barry, Sir Edward | 49, 220 |
| Barsac | 61 |
| Barton, Mr. | 16 |
| Beaujolais | 64 |
| Beaune | 64 |
| Bede | 12 |
| Beckford, Mr. | 27 |
| Benicarlo | 96 |
| Bodenheim | 148 |
| Bosc | 22 |
| Brande, Mr. | 34, 35, 37, 113 |
| Brauneberger | 150 |
| Bremer, Frederica | 175, 177 |
| Brinton, Dr. | 40 |
| Bronner | 51 |
| Bucellas | 122 |
| Buda | 156 |
| Burgundy | 48, 63, 67, 74 |
| Busby, Dr. | 42 |
| Busby, Mr. | 200 |
| Byron, Lord | 178 |
| Cœcuban | 165 |
| Calcavello | 123 |
| Calliste | 177 |
| Canary | 53, 136 |

| | PAGE |
|---|---|
| Cape | 196 |
| Carlowitz | 156 |
| Catawba | 190 |
| Cato | 45 |
| Chablis | 66 |
| Chambertin | 64 |
| Champagne, 41, 53, 67, 74, | 76, 210, 232 |
| Chaptal | 2, 50 |
| Château Lafitte | 58 |
| Château Latour | 58 |
| Château Margaux | 58, 61, 212 |
| Château Yquem | 61, 212 |
| Chiarello | 166 |
| Chiavenna | 162 |
| Cicero | 3, 47, 231 |
| Claret | 59, 227 |
| Clos Vougeôt | 19, 64 |
| Cobbett, Mr. | 24, 26 |
| Colares Port | 123 |
| Columella | 6, 45 |
| Constantia | 198 |
| Corinthe | 179 |
| Corton | 64 |
| Côte Rotie | 63 |
| Creuznacher | 149 |
| Daily Telegraph | 161 |
| Democritus | 45 |
| Denman, Mr. | 51 |
| D'Urfey, Thomas | 100, 180 |
| Diodorus | 174 |
| Domesday Book | 12 |
| Dunlop, Mr. Graham | 156 |
| Ebro Port | 210 |
| Elbe Sherry | 209 |
| Erasmus | 48 |
| Erlauer | 156 |
| Falernian | 2, 47, 165 |
| Family Grocer, The, | 206, 211, 212 |

U

PAGE

Florence....................... 166
Forrester, Mr.   50, 115, 117, 120
Forsyth, Mr. ................... 28
French Reds ................... 205
Frontignan................. 53, 86
Fumarium, The .............. 4
Galen .................... 45, 179
Geisenheim.................... 147
Gira ......................... 170
Gladstone, Mr. ... 69, 71, 72, 74
Gmelin ....................... 36
Goldeck....................... 159
Graff ......................... 51
Gros Wardein................. 156
Hahnemann, Dr. ........... ˙33
Hales ......................... 13
Hamburg Sherry ...... 205, 209
Haut Brion.................... 61
Henderson, Dr.......49, 155, 176
Hermitage.................. 62, 68
Hinterhaus ........ ........... 147
Hippocrates .............. 45, 178
Hochheim .................... 148
Hock ......................... 153
Holdsworth Dr. .............. 40
Home, John ................. 114
Homer ............. 1, 44, 174
Homer's Nectar .............. 174
Horace ...... 2, 3, 4, 6, 47, 232
Howell ....................... 136
Humboldt, Baron ........... 10
Hume, David................. 114
Hunt, Leigh ................. 167
Ingelheim .................... 147
Isabella ...................... 190
Ithaca, red wine of........... 180
Jerrold, Douglas.............. 29
Johannisberg ......... 19, 146
Johannisberg Claus........... 146
Johnson, Dr. ................. 114
Josephshöfer ................ 150
Jullien................. 50, 66, 81
Jurors' Report, 139, 153, 157,
            161, 163, 170, 186, 201
Juvenal ...................... 47
Kirner Schmisser ........... 149

PAGE

Kirwan, Mr. ................. 210
Kletzinsky .................... 152
Koborn ...................... 185
Lachrymæ Christi ........... 166
Laubenheim ................. 148
Lawrence, Mr. .............. 20
Leoville ...................... 61
Liebfraumilch................. 148
Liebig .................... 78, 152
Lisbon ....................... 122
Lissa ......................... 170
Loudon, Mr. ............. 14, 20
Lunel ........................ 86
McCulloch, Dr.... 32, 33, 40, 50
Macon ....................... 64
Madeira .................. 54, 130
Mago ......................... 45
Malmsey ...... 53, 99, 135, 174
Malmsey Madeira ........... 130
Mangiaguerra ................ 166
Manzanilla.................... 95
Marcobrunner................. 147
Maronean .................... 176
Marsala ...................... 169
Martial, 47, 102, 165, 174, 231
Martyn, Professor ........... 14
Masdeu ...................... 85
Massandra ................... 185
Medical Times and Gazette... 206
Meursault .................... 66
Menes........................ 156
Methuen Treaty ......... 68, 109
Michaux...................... 10
Miller, Mr.................... 18
Modenese .................... 167
Montefiascone ........... 53, 166
Montepulciano ............... 167
Montilla...................... 94
Montrachet................... 66
Montserrat ................... 167
Monzinger ................... 149
Moselle ...................... 150
Mountain .................... 95
Mouton .................. 58, 61
Muscadine ................... 167
Muscatel..................... 166

| | PAGE |
|---|---|
| Nasco | 170 |
| Neuberger | 150 |
| Neufchâtel | 162 |
| Niersteiner | 148 |
| Norheimer | 149 |
| Odenburg | 156 |
| Ofner | 156 |
| Oidium, The, 86, 103, 124, 131, 137, | 168 |
| Oligsberger | 150 |
| Oliveira, Mr. Benjamin | 70 |
| Olivier | 9 |
| Oppenheim | 148 |
| Orvieto | 166 |
| Ovid | 47 |
| Paguierre | 50 |
| Pallas | 9, 185 |
| Paris, Dr. | 41 |
| Passum | 174 |
| Patera, The | 5 |
| Patin | 48 |
| Paumier | 48 |
| Pausilippo | 166 |
| Paxarété | 96 |
| Pereira, Dr. | 40 |
| Peruvian Madeira | 137 |
| Phocylides | 44 |
| Plato | 45, 48 |
| Plautus | 4 |
| Pliny, 22, 48, 174, 176, 179, | 231 |
| Pommard | 64 |
| Pontac | 199 |
| Port | 54, 111, 225 |
| Porta | 194 |
| Porter, Mr. G. R. | 214 |
| Pouilly | 66 |
| Pramnian | 174, 176 |
| Prout, Dr. | 152 |
| Pythagoras | 178 |
| Rauzan | 61 |
| Redding, Mr. Cyrus, 50, 62, 68, 142, 215, | 220 |
| Rhyton, The | 5 |
| Ridley's Circular | 207 |
| Reislinger | 148 |
| Rivesaltes | 86 |
| | PAGE |
| Romanée Conti | 64 |
| Rota Tinto | 95 |
| Roussillon | 60 |
| Roxheimer | 149 |
| Rudesheim | 146 |
| Ruskin, Mr. | 214 |
| Sack | 97, 136 |
| St. Emelion | 59, 61 |
| St. Elie | 177 |
| St. George | 156 |
| Salces | 86 |
| Salernitan | 166 |
| Salquener | 162 |
| Santorin | 177 |
| Sauterne | 61 |
| Scham | 51 |
| Scharlachberg | 148, 149 |
| Scuppernong | 190 |
| Shaw, Mr. | 51, 71, 209, 214 |
| Sherry, 54, 92, 93, 105, 212, | 225 |
| Shiraz | 53, 183 |
| Sibthorp, Dr. | 8 |
| Sickler, Dr. | 11 |
| Soleras | 95 |
| South African | 196, 204, 209 |
| Spanish Reds | 96, 205 |
| Sparkling Catawba | 190 |
| Sparkling Hock | 151 |
| Sparkling Moselle | 151 |
| Sparkling Vöslauer | 159 |
| Steinberg (Austrian) | 159 |
| Steinberg (Rhine) | 147 |
| Stein Wines | 148 |
| Strabo | 174 |
| Tent | 95 |
| Termo | 123 |
| Thera | 177 |
| Tibullus | 4, 47 |
| Times, The | 160 |
| Tinta | 130 |
| Tokay | 53, 155 |
| Tovey, Mr. | 50, 212, 215 |
| Val de Penas | 96 |
| Valteline | 162 |
| Varro | 47 |
| Verrachia | 166 |

| PAGE | | PAGE |
|---|---|---|
| Vidonia ......................... 134 | Volnay ......................... 64 |
| Vino d'Asti .................. 167 | Vôslau ......................... 159 |
| Vino de Pasto.................. 93 | William of Malmesbury...... 12 |
| Vino Greco..................... 166 | Wine of Bacchus ........... 177 |
| Vino Santo..................... 177 | Wine of Helbon............. 185 |
| Vino vergine ................. 166 | Wine of Night ............... 177 |
| Vins de Graves ........... 59, 61 | Wine of Tyre.................. 185 |
| Vinum coctum .............. 53 | Winzenheimer ............... 149 |
| Vinum cotto ................. 53 | Yvorne ........................ 162 |
| Vinum Rhæticum ........... 47 | Zeltinger....................... 150 |
| Virgil............................ 47 | Zeno ........................... 47 |

## MALT LIQUORS, &c.

| | |
|---|---|
| Ale-connors ................. 244 | Ives, Dr...................... 262 |
| Barley......................... 251 | Loudon, Mr. .................. 258 |
| Belon ......................... 237 | Malt ........................... 250 |
| Brande, Mr. .................. 260 | Maton, Dr..................... 262 |
| Brewing ...................... 245 | Orgeat ........................ 238 |
| Chapman, Dr. ............... 262 | Paris, Dr. ..................... 262 |
| Charlemagne ................. 240 | Pereira, Dr...... .............. 262 |
| Curmi.......................... 237 | Pliny ....................238, 251 |
| Desroches, Dr. ............... 262 | Posca .......................... 238 |
| Diodorus Siculus.............. 238 | Statutes ................243, 256 |
| Dion Cassius ................. 238 | Still, Dr. John ............... 242 |
| Einhof ........................ 253 | Tacitus ...................... . 238 |
| Harwood ..................... 248 | Theophrastus .................. 238 |
| Herodotus .................... 237 | Thomson, Professor ......... 251 |
| Hippocrates................... 252 | Willis, Dr. .................... 263 |
| Hops .......................... 254 | Zythus ........................ 238 |

## SPIRITS, &c.

| | |
|---|---|
| Albucasis ..................... 269 | Lavoisier...................... 274 |
| Alcohol ....................... 273 | Liqueurs ....................... 281 |
| Arrack ........................ 272 | Lully, Raymond ...... 269, 280 |
| Brandy .................. 272, 279 | Morewood ..................... 269 |
| Compounds.................... 281 | Proof Spirit.................... 281 |
| Corn Spirit.................... 273 | Rum ....................272, 278 |
| Geber .......................... 268 | Spirit of Wine................. 273 |
| Gin ...................... 273, 275 | Villeneuve, Arnauld de ...... 268 |
| Hollands.................. 273, 275 | Whiskey ............... 273, 275 |

## CONCLUSION.

| | |
|---|---|
| Byron, Lord .................. 284 | Tovey, Mr. ................... 283 |
| Dickens, Charles .... ....... 287 | Valedictory..................... 288 |

www.ingramcontent.com/pod-product-compliance
Lightning Source LLC
Chambersburg PA
CBHW020500270326
41926CB00008B/688